RELENTLESS GROWTH

Cultivating
a Chef's Mindset
for Professional
Fulfillment

FRANCK DESPLECHIN

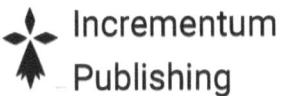 Incrementum
Publishing

RELENTLESS GROWTH:
Cultivating a Chef's Mindset for Professional Fulfillment

Paperback ISBN: 979-8-218-73792-4

First Paperback Edition: October 2025

Edited by: Sabrina Butler, Unpolished Words
Edited by: Carmen Smith and Elise Smith, Wordy Wives
Cover by: Make Your Mark Publishing Solutions
Layout by: Make Your Mark Publishing Solutions

TO:

_____

because growth lives in your mindset. The rest follows.

FROM:

_____

AUTHOR SIGNATURE:

_____

To Suzie Yang,

You believed in me before I knew how to believe in myself. You are, without question, the kindest, most generous soul I have ever known, with a generosity that feels like it belongs to another world. Your belief in me and your friendship have shaped my journey in ways words will never fully capture. This book is a testament to the impact you have had on my life and the incredible person you are.

CONTENTS

FOREWORD

Mise en Appétit... (For Success)

From Jean-Luc Rabanel, Chef Owner of Les Maisons Rabanel, Maître Cuisinier de France, Chef of the year 2008 in the guide Gault-Millau, 2** Michelin stars in 2009, 5 toques in the guide Gault-Millau since 2012 (Top 15 best restaurants in France)

Welcome to a world where cooking is not just about the recipes but about a true journey of personal development! This book, crafted by Franck Desplechin—my former chef, pastry chef, and collaborator—invites us to dive into a flavorful adventure of growth. Who would have thought that preparing a dish could teach lessons in resilience and creativity?

In Relentless Growth: Cultivating a Chef's Mindset for Professional Fulfillment, Franck offers us far more than a simple culinary guide. He shares his unique vision of gastronomy, where every dish becomes a metaphor. Here, every plate served is a chance to learn, and every failure in the kitchen is just a step toward a masterpiece. As Franck reminds us, sometimes we need to step out of our comfort zones to taste the delights of the unknown. After all, who said that the fear of burning a quiche couldn't lead to a life-changing revelation? Each chapter in this book explores the challenges of the culinary world and the invaluable lessons that arise from them, highlighting how every mistake, every failed dish, is an opportunity to learn and an invitation to reinvent oneself.

Franck, I remember our time together—when we earned two Michelin stars and I was named Chef of the year with 5 toques and a 19/20 rating by Gault & Millau—thanks in part to your passion and creativity in the kitchen, which were contagious for the entire team. As a chef, you didn't just follow recipes, you turned those recipes into works of art with your boldness and sensitivity. As a leader, you inspired those around you to bring out their best, creating an environment where everyone felt valued and motivated. Your ability to handle the pressure of service while maintaining a sense of camaraderie and enthusiasm was remarkable. The qualities you embodied then and now share in this book are essential in every aspect of professional life, not just in the kitchen.

For those of you reading this, you're about to embark on an adventure full of flavor and inspiration toward the best version of yourself! Be prepared to grow—and to act. This book will push you toward both, whether you are a young professional looking for your own recipe for success or a seasoned leader wanting to spice up your career. Franck offers practical strate-gies to develop a growth mindset, to embrace challenges, and to turn aspirations into tangible results. He invites all of us to see the kitchen as a space for experimentation, where boldness and curiosity are essential ingredients for every dish.

As you read, you'll discover that, just like in cooking, every step matters, and every ingredient plays a role in the grand rec-ipe of life. Franck's reflections on teamwork, time management, and the power of passion remind us that success is not measured by achievements alone but by the path taken to reach those achievements.

So, tie your napkin around your neck and let yourself be swept up in this captivating journey.

Accept the invitation to push beyond your limits, feed your ambitions, and savor every moment of your professional growth.

To Franck, with all my friendship,

Jean-Luc RABANEL

UNVEILING THE ART OF GROWTH

I remember standing at the edge of my comfort zone, wondering whether to take that next step. Fear? Yes, it was definitely there, but so was the quiet urge to push beyond what I thought I was capable of.

Growth is not something that just happens to you; it is something you create with intention. It starts with that tiny spark—the one that tells you there is more waiting for you if you are willing to step into the unknown.

I remember that day like it was yesterday. I was contemplating the idea of moving for my job one more time, but this move felt different. I had lived in my *fare* in Bora-Bora for over two years. The bungalow was comfortable, considering I was on an island of eleven square miles in the middle of the Pacific Ocean. My routine was set; I knew the place, the people, the job expected of me, and the rhythm of my life inside and out. But here was this opportunity—one that could change everything.

There was only one *minor* problem: I am French. I did not speak a word of English, and the job opportunity was in Hawaii. I knew this opportunity was the next step of my career, but the gravity of what it meant sank in almost immediately. Taking this job would entail far more than advancing my skills and gaining experience—it meant uprooting my entire life and challenging myself. It meant leaving behind the familiar and stepping into the unknown of a completely different country, a different culture, and a kitchen where the language, both spoken and written, was different.

Fear gripped me. I had worked hard to get where I was— building a reputation, establishing relationships, and carving out a space in the culinary scene of this well-established resort. I was comfortable too; I knew the landscape and I was happy with my current situation. But truth be told, my ambition was starting to catch up with me; the island was starting to feel too small for my dreams.

The night before I decided to entertain this opportunity, I was swinging in my hammock overlooking the beautiful lagoon of Bora-Bora. I let myself imagine life in Hawaii—the culture, the people, the career opportunity, the potential of turning this page and starting a life-changing chapter. There was something there for me, I knew it, but only if I was willing to step forward. That night, standing at the edge of that decision, I realized growth always came from embracing the unknown, not from staying in my eleven-mile comfort zone.

I went to bed that night but I couldn't sleep, so why wait? *Just go for it now*, I thought. So at 3 a.m., I got out of bed and sent out my resume and recommendation letter, alongside my formal application. And that was it. While everyone slept, I took my first step toward what I knew would be a challenging, daunting journey—one that would inevitably stretch me beyond my current limits.

The process was pretty standard from that moment on, but even standard processes were unsettling since I didn't yet speak the language required to get the job. My first and only language was French. Nevertheless, my first scheduled interview was with the Executive Chef and the Director of Food & Beverage of the resort in Hawaii, and it would be in English. It was what they called a "behavioral interview," which I was completely clueless about at the time. Even though I was a chef trained to handle tough situations under a lot of pressure, this interview was something else. My hands were sweating, I was unsure, I felt incompetent, and yet, I was determined to see it through.

Total disaster! I failed so badly and barely made it to the third question. About one hour later, though, I got a call. It was the Executive Chef of the resort offering me a second chance. He gave me the entire interview questionnaire in French and told me I would get another interview the next day, first thing in the morning. I accepted and told him I would be ready.

It was 6 p.m. when I hung up; the interview was scheduled for 8 a.m.—I had fourteen hours to prepare. But first, dinner service.

I got back to my bungalow around 10:30 p.m. that night, with just nine and a half hours left to get ready for a full interview in English. This was over a decade ago, so Google translate was the best tool available. I responded to each of the eight questions in French, translated them into English, and then transcribed them back to the questionnaire in order to somewhat memorize them. I finished this process around 7 a.m., just in time to take a shower and get ready for the second, and probably last, chance to pass this interview.

I was feeling nervous but ready. I had lined up all the questions in order with their answers on the desk in front of me. But the first question immediately threw me off; they started with question #6, and I could barely understand anything they were saying. I blamed the resort's Wi-Fi signal and asked them to repeat the questions a few times, capturing the key words in English as they did so. I had to answer the correct question. After I regained my footing, I read my corresponding answer and tried to speak in a way that didn't clue them in to the fact that I was reading. After just four questions, they asked to stop the interview and told me they would be in touch.

Talk about a nerve-racking situation! After the longest two hours of my life, the Executive Chef called to tell me I was moving on to the next step of the process: an interview with the director of human resources. Due to the nature of the position, I would also get a chance to connect with the resort's general manager. And I thought the hardest was behind me...it wasn't. This was uncharted territory—new language, new culture, and stakes that felt higher than ever. I did what I could to prepare, but the nerves hit just as hard. Maybe harder.

Two days later, I had my call with the director of human resources, and, lucky me, she loved talking so much that all I had to do was listen and pretend I understood. So I passed with flying colors on that one. Next up was the general manager, and I knew I wouldn't be able to fake it; after all, he was the general manager. I had to find a way to convince him I was the right person for the job—minus the ability to speak, understand, or write the language. As mentioned before: minor details.

The night before my interview with the general manager, I was informed that it had to be postponed to the following week. I felt great about that, like I had nailed it even though it hadn't happened yet. The following week arrived and I received another email. The general manager would have to reschedule once more, so I was to receive an offer letter that day. I couldn't believe what had just happened! I had gotten a job offer to be Executive Pastry Chef of a luxury resort in Hawaii!

My mind replayed the past few weeks. The night in my hammock, my decision to apply for the job, stumbling through only half-understood interviews, the all-nighters I took to prepare, and now this—all because of a bulletproof mindset, a refusal to accept failure, an obsessive unwillingness to give up, and, let's be honest, an awful lot of luck. I signed the offer, and I was on my way to Hawaii on a sponsored Visa.

Growth as an art demands that we look at life differently, that we see the beauty in failure or find the lesson in struggle. The Art of Growth, as I like to call it, does not wait for us to be ready; it calls to us and catches us by surprise when we're unsure, insecure, or fearful. This is not theoretical ideology; it is practical, transformative, and, most importantly, it is raw. It is what helped me turn moments of doubt into defining breakthroughs. And I would like to share it with you.

I am not here to give you all the answers. I am here to guide you as you uncover your own. This journey is yours, and it starts when you awaken your own growth mindset and pursue it relentlessly wherever it leads. But before you accept the journey, I want you to hear this vital truth: growth is a creative, ongoing process rather than a finite destination. I invite you to read that last sentence again as you have a long road ahead of you. You must comprehend there will be no destination.

Depending on your stage of life, that will either come as good news or bad news. Young professionals, particularly in hospitality, are looking for more than just career advancement—they're seeking purpose, growth, and fulfillment in their roles. Older professionals, the current leaders in this field, tend to get stuck in their familiar ways. Growth is the catalyst for each of us to rethink the traditional expectations of the workforce and adapt to meet the needs of those shaping our future.

The next generation of hospitality workers and leaders places a higher value on learning and growth than on traditional perks. Many of you are actively seeking opportunities to develop, often willing to invest your own time and resources into training, education, and meaningful career experiences. When companies genuinely support your growth, you are more likely to stay, contribute fully, and lead with purpose. You are not driven by titles or promotions alone; you are driven by progress, impact, and fulfillment.

You are stepping into an industry that can feel at odds with your values. After years of global disruption, uncertainty, and instability, the desire for balance is not a luxury; it is a lifeline. Yet hospitality, with its relentless pace and unpredictable hours, doesn't make that balance easy. Still, your pursuit of it is a powerful redefinition of what it means to succeed, not a lack of drive. You are choosing purpose over pressure, and that takes courage.

At the same time, you are operating in a new kind of spotlight. Online reviews, social media feedback, and ever-shifting guest expectations have added layers of pressure that were not there before. You are expected to deliver five-star service, anticipate unspoken needs, and respond instantly to criticism; all while growing into your own as a leader.

These challenges are often misunderstood, and so are you. But here is what I know: You are not afraid of hard work. You are simply unwilling to sacrifice your well-being for outdated ideas of success. That shift is not just valid; it is necessary. And it is up to the rest of us to understand it, embrace it, and help you thrive within it. Because when we invest in your growth and your well-being, we don't just build better teams, we build a better future for this entire industry. That is what this book is here to support. That is the transformation we have a chance to create together. And it starts with accepting that growth has no set destination.

The future of hospitality depends on how well we respond to this generational shift. To this day, there remains an unfortunate, chronic challenge within the hospitality industry: a systemic lack of prioritization for ongoing, structured training and mentorship. Far too many employers rely on the unpredictable nature of on-the-job learning, which often leaves employees navigating their way through inconsistent standards and varied levels of guidance. Through my work in hospitality over twenty-six years, I have witnessed this challenge and continue to see it in so many workplaces. This inconsistency gradually destroys the very foundation on which true professional growth should be built.

Today's hospitality education programs, while valuable, often fall short of bridging the gap between theory and the real world.

The dynamic nature of the industry makes staying relevant a challenge, often leaving graduates unprepared for the demands of their first job. Theories can help, but they rarely equip students for the high-paced, high-pressure environments that define hospitality, especially in the luxury segment, where guest expectations are at their peak. The rigors of the job can quickly overwhelm those entering the field, which is why structured mentorship is essential to bridge the gap. But, industry-wide, we're far from this ideal, and the gap between hospitality training and the real-word demands of the job remains.

Many young professionals who make it through this gap get promoted a few years later—not because they have been prepared or guided but because they have proven to be strong individual performers. And so the cycle begins: promoting without leadership training. This leads to systemic weaknesses in team dynamics and organizational culture. The belief that high performers or long-tenured employees automatically make great leaders is a persistent misconception. While they may excel in their roles, leadership requires a different set of skills: empathy, communication, mentorship, and the ability to inspire others. Without guidance, these new leaders are left to figure this out alone. Some may improve through trial and error but at the cost of poor morale, high turnover, and inconsistent guest experiences. And when they rise to even higher roles, the cycle repeats, producing leaders who have never truly learned what it means to be servant leaders. This is the dangerous game that we—and the leaders before us—have been playing. We have not yet taken accountability for the culture we're creating; if not now, when?

Let's talk about the other leaders too—the ones who, after years of success and dedication, suddenly feel unfulfilled or stuck, no matter their age or title. If this is you, you know you're responsible for holding the whole operation together. Yet the moment your performance dips, you are overlooked, micromanaged, or written off. Despite your achievements, you are searching for something deeper. And what you need isn't rocket science. You need inspiration. You need a boss who cares, not just about your performance but about your growth. Even if that means supporting you through a transition, even if it means you're moving on. That is what real leadership looks like, supporting people, especially during uncertain times. We have to be willing to listen, not just to hear you out but to truly understand. Leadership, like growth, has no destination—it is a continuous journey of learning and evolving. No matter how much you have achieved, the opportunity to reignite your passion is always within reach.

I have believed in the power of hospitality for decades, both for those who live it and those who receive it. As a young cook, I used to think the magic was in the dish. I did not know any better. And in those early years, the dishes were not even mine. I followed directions. I honored the vision of a chef I respected. That was the job, and I loved it. When the time finally came to create my own dish, I was criticized. Judged. And it stung. But with an open mind, I learned to push boundaries, and I grew.

A career in hospitality teaches you that the real magic is not just in mastering technique or knowing the perfect wine pairing, it is also in the journey itself—the long hours, the discipline, the creativity, the failures, the people. Hospitality will challenge you, shape you, and teach you how to evolve. Most of all, it will teach you about yourself, how to push beyond what you thought was possible, adapt to every turn, and embrace your next evolution.

I have witnessed firsthand how personal growth, resilience, and a relentless mindset are critical to success in this industry. As someone who's spent years mastering culinary arts and navigating the complexities of hospitality through food and beverage, I understand the unique challenges and opportunities this field offers.

You may be stepping into hospitality with dreams and ambitions, but also with uncertainty about your path forward. Maybe you are feeling unfulfilled, stuck, or disengaged with your own craft. Maybe you're wondering how to grow not just in skills, but in mindset, resilience, and personal well-being. Or maybe you are desperately pursuing career fulfillment and do not know where to start. Keep being aware of these feelings; write them down! Practicing self-reflection is important, healthy, and vital to growth.

This industry is not just a job; it is a journey of self-discovery and relentless self-improvement. So, how do we turn challenges into opportunities, setbacks into comebacks, and moments of doubt into moments of breakthrough? There is no doubt in my mind that anyone who adopts this mindset—this relentless pursuit of growth—will reach career fulfillment. It's not just a possibility; it is the inevitable result of committing to the Art of Growth.

As a well-established chef, I know what it means to get "slammed" at the pass during a heavy dinner rush, the constant pressure of perfecting every dish one guest at a time, the sleepless nights, and the verbal abuse and bullying that still exist in some kitchens. But I also know the exhilaration of pushing through as a team, of learning something new daily, of seeing your team succeed, and of growing through every challenging opportunity. It is those lessons, born from the daily grind of hospitality and re- fined in the heat of the kitchen, that we'll walk through together over the course of this book.

It is time to thrive and break out of the vicious cycle of sur- vival, and it is clear to me that those who adapt, who learn, and who commit to self-improvement will be the ones who lead the way forward. So many individuals—especially in hospitality— are searching for more than just a job. This book is about far more than teaching certain skills or offering career advice; it is about transforming lives. When we adopt the mindset of relentless growth, we begin to approach everything differently. Pursuing growth becomes intrinsic to our identity.

I strongly believe the principles of this book—resilience, growth, and the relentless pursuit of both—are universal, and the lessons I've learned in hospitality can be applied to any career or life path. The stories I share are real and raw. I've had to work through the emotional toll of missing a family funeral while leading a pastry team on a remote island. I've had to push past rejection in pursuit of a Michelin star. I hope my stories remind you that growth is always within reach. I hope they serve as a call to action: you have the power to shape your own path, no matter where or, more importantly, when you decide to start.

In all my years as Executive Chef, I found myself repeatedly witnessing the same struggle in each of the properties I was hired for. Ambition without guidance. Potential slipping through the cracks, not from a lack of effort, but from a missing sense of direction. It was impossible for me to ignore the disconnect between where we were as an industry and where we were meant to be. The challenge was rarely in the work itself; it was in the silence left behind, where purpose used to be. It was in those moments when I knew I needed to do things differently and made the conscious decision to be part of the solution. Not the solution my bosses wanted me to focus on, but the solution to a systemic problem—workplace culture.

From 2015 to 2020, I was stunned by the overwhelming absence of healthy culture, accountability, and structured training in every kitchen I encountered. There was, instead, a deep-rooted culture of absenteeism, where team members did whatever they wanted with little to no guidance or accountability. The kitchen lacked direction and clear objectives. Neither growth nor striving for excellence were prioritized; each day was about surviving, then scrambling to prepare for the next day of surviving. This chaotic environment eroded any sense of teamwork or pride in the craft. Although I couldn't believe what I was witnessing, it became clear to me that jobs in this industry weren't just about cooking, and maybe they never were. Maybe hospitality has always been about igniting and then reigniting purpose, setting the foundation for a culture of leadership, where expectations were clear and everyone had the tools and direction they needed to thrive.

But in the midst of all this, I kept asking myself, How can I fix a broken culture when I still need growth myself? I knew that leadership was not about having all the answers but about being determined enough to ask the right questions, especially the tough ones, which is hard when you are at the highest position in the kitchen. Who do you possibly ask?

It became clear to me that before I could inspire change in others, I needed to continue my own journey of growth, but this time with an understanding that it would directly impact those around me. This new journey was not about improving my technical skills as a chef—it was about strengthening my mindset, expanding my capacity to lead, and learning how to create an environment that fostered genuine development.

The fear of failing in this endeavor took on a threatening shape. *What if I fail? What if I let the team down?* These thoughts weighed heavily on me until I remembered that setbacks were not signs of defeat; they were the most critical parts of the process. A process I needed to embrace fully. Each challenge, I decided, would be an opportunity to continue learning and growing, and this shift in my perspective was vital for the journey ahead. I had to embrace failure as a teacher, not an enemy. I had to strengthen my growth mindset to build resilience not only in myself but in the culture I wanted to create as well.

The hospitality industry is at a pivotal juncture, and the time to act is now! We must fill the gaps caused by insufficient training and stop focusing on performance at the expense of culture. Every step we take on this journey shapes who we become and the impact we leave behind. Let that sink in for a moment. Whether you are an emerging professional or a seasoned leader, there is a real opportunity for transformation—both internal and external.

But acting now doesn't mean rushing toward a quick fix or seeking instant results. True growth, both personal and professional, requires a lot of patience and an acceptance that there are no shortcuts. The journey of self-discovery, learning, and change is long, but it leads to deeper fulfillment and career success. By embracing the process and committing to the work, we can lead with confidence and instill a culture of excellence, and we might just enjoy the ride that much more if we accept the ups and down along the way. So, whether you are just starting out in the hospitality industry or you're looking to reconnect with your purpose, now is the time to take that first step.

Stay curious, define your vision, and align your actions to bring out the best version of yourself. It is your daily choices—the small improvements, the incremental changes—that accumulate over time and lead to real transformation. Success is rooted far more in how we think and adapt than in what we do. This is the long journey to growth—and it's worth every step.

I have experienced firsthand the highs and lows of an industry that tests not only skills but mental fortitude, from my early days in Michelin-star-rated restaurants in France, where the pressure was constant and the demands were unrelenting, to stepping into management and executive roles where culture and leadership were shockingly absent. Throughout these experiences, I never stopped working on the most important part of my success—my mindset.

I understood early that success entailed more than hard work—though I have paid my dues in that regard. I realized success also required thinking differently, evolving, and relentlessly pushing forward, no matter the challenge. When I faced adversity, I chose to transform it, consistently focusing on personal growth as the key to lasting achievement. I intentionally cultivated a growth mindset, and I like to believe that this deep, personal commitment to transform myself from within has set me apart throughout my journey. I made and continue to make this commitment, and I want to share that process with you. I have lived it and refined it, and now it is your time to take the stage. Your time to unlock the potential within you and achieve career fulfillment through relentless dedication to your personal and professional growth.

The path to success begins the moment you choose to believe in your own capacity to evolve. Once a chef, always a chef. And just like cooking, I approach growth as an art form, not just a concept. The opportunity for growth does not wait for the perfect moment; it arrives when you are least prepared, demanding that you rise to the occasion. When you're shuffled to an unfamiliar kitchen station right before service on one of the busiest days of the year, that's the moment it shows up, because sometimes pressure is the teacher you did not ask for but needed.

The journey of growth is long, and there is no finish line—only the next step forward, then the next, then the next. But the journey itself is worth it.

Each chapter of this book will guide you through the steps of developing a growth mindset. It starts with defining your vision and fostering curiosity; these two things set the foundation for self-growth. As you move forward on this lifelong journey, you will learn how to balance ambition with patience, how to thrive under pressure, and how to overcome the inevitable setbacks along the way.

This is my invitation into a new world: a world where you are capable of more, a world where you are willing to step into the unknown, knowing you'll grow through it.

This is your journey—own it, and watch as your life transforms before your eyes.

CHAPTER 1

THE CURIOUS LENS: DEFINE YOUR VISION

In France, there is a saying that "curiosity begins at home," and that was absolutely true for me. After all, home is the first environment where we observe, learn, and explore the world around us. Home is where our early experiences shape how we interact with life.

I grew up in Châteaulin, a charming town nestled in the heart of Brittany, France, known for its location along the stunning Aulne River. Today, the town has lost its beauty and seductiveness—at least to me. But back then, it offered a blend of natural beauty and rich Breton culture, with its scenic riverside views and rolling green hills. The town exuded a sense of history and tradition, its quaint streets lined with local markets, bakeries, and cafes offering authentic Breton specialties such as crêpes and cider. Châteaulin was a quieter town compared to the bustling coastal cities, giving it a peaceful and authentic atmosphere that reflected the slower pace of life in rural Brittany.

Both my parents shaped my earliest memories of food and cooking. My mother, the heart of the household, spent hours in the kitchen every day, crafting comforting traditional dishes. She wasn't interested in impressing anyone with her cooking—she was focused on feeding her family, nurturing us with flavors that felt familiar and warm. From the veal blanquette and beef bourguignon to the mussels with pomme frites and her insatiable buckwheat crepes—the true masterpiece: thin and thick all at once, and impeccably golden, with the perfect balance of buttery crispness and tender softness. Despite the countless hours spent in the kitchen, my mom made it look effortless. But even as a child, I could sense the love and dedication she poured into every meal.

My father, on the other hand, was not in the kitchen as often, but when he was, he had his own way of doing things. Unlike my mom's consistent, day-to-day comfort food, my dad would step in during the holidays to create something more elaborate, special dinners meant to dazzle. When he cooked on these occasions, the kitchen became his stage and the meal a performance. I watched him closely in these moments, following recipes it seemed he had never followed before. I was fascinated by his ability to make food look beautiful, almost as if he were creating art on the plate. Together, my parents unknowingly sparked my early curiosity about cooking. From my mom, I learned the value of tradition and patience, and the importance of comforting flavors that bring family together. From my dad, I discovered that food could be more than sustenance; it could be an experience, a way to create moments of joy and celebration.

In those early days, I did not yet understand how these influences would shape my future, but I felt drawn to the kitchen. I didn't participate in cooking as much as you would think—I was too shy to try and a bit afraid of what others might think of me. All I knew was that I was particularly curious about it. I watched it happen from the corner of my eyes—always learning, always seeking out new information to add to my growing observations—viewing my small world through what I now call the "Curious Lens."

1.1 CURIOSITY OVER EXPECTATIONS

Sometimes life places you at a crossroads between the expectations of those around you and the pull of something deeper—your own passion. It is not uncommon to feel the weight of well-meaning advice from family, close friends, or loved ones pushing you toward what they believe is best for you. But here is the truth: no one else can fully understand and embrace your inner drive, nor experience the excitement that comes when you allow curiosity to take the lead.

Your passion deserves space to grow. And that growth begins with curiosity—being bold enough to explore, even when the world around you and those who claim to know you better than you know yourself might not understand. Do not settle for the answers you have been given or the paths others expect you to follow. Instead, ask more, dig deeper, and follow the sparks that excite you. Every time you choose to foster your curiosity, you are investing in your future self. Believe me, you will thank yourself later!

What if the thing you are passionate about, the thing that lights you up, opens the door to something far greater than you could ever imagine? The only way to find out is to follow that spark and give yourself permission to explore it fully. That is the essence of the Curious Lens—giving yourself the right to dream and explore. Your drive and your passion make up your life's compass, and your curiosity is the needle pointing you forward. It is so much easier to take ownership of your journey when you entertain an idea or pursuit that makes you feel alive. At this stage of exploration, there is absolutely no reason to be afraid, so let curiosity guide you. Trust it, nurture it, and see where it takes you. I know from experience that the path of curiosity may not be the most straightforward, but I can assure you it leads to discovery, growth, and, ultimately, some level of fulfillment.

Choosing curiosity over expectation is not designed to be easy. In kitchens, most people settle for mastering the how—how to execute, how to move fast, how to stay out of trouble. But the real shift in growth happens when you start asking why. Why this method? Why that ingredient? Why now? As my parents will tell you, I have been asking these questions my whole life. They probably wished for one peaceful meal without me interrogating them about the recipe. And my obsession with asking why didn't stop there. As an apprentice, I drove my chefs nuts with my endless questions. But that so-called "annoyance" became my edge. Because when you chase the why behind everything, you stop mimicking and you start understanding. Practicing curiosity means turning every task into a chance to learn, not just perform. That is how you build real knowledge, one thoughtful question at a time.

The moment you commit to that path, something will shift. Opportunities and experiences that you couldn't have predicted, doors that never would've opened will begin to reveal themselves once you leave the confines of what others expect of you. Along the way, you will grow—both personally and professionally—in ways that the "safe" path would never have allowed. Trust yourself to believe in your own vision, and give yourself permission to pursue something that feels right for you, even if it's not conventional. The decision I made decades ago to unapologetically follow my curiosity has shaped everything I've done since, and it continues to remind me that choosing curiosity means choosing a life of growth and authenticity.

I am sure that many of you walk, drive, or take public transportation to work, listening to your favorite music, trying to get the motivation to show up for one more day, clock in, go through the motions, and clock out. It is easy to fall into the routine of doing what's expected, staying within the confines of what has worked before. But if you want growth, purpose, and a reason to wake up excited, choose curiosity over expectation; curiosity is the key that unlocks it all.

If you're seeking meaning and fulfillment over a paycheck, if you want a lifeline out of burnout, be careful of the all-too-familiar cycle of simply doing what is necessary without feeling any real connection to your work. That is a death trap. But you can avoid it by making a conscious decision to free yourself from the rigid path of what *should* happen. You can take control of your own narrative when you shift from expectation to curiosity. This journey does not belong to anyone but you! Curiosity is the beginning, but vision—well, that's what keeps you going.

1.2 WHERE CLARITY MATTERS MOST

In the pursuit of professional growth, the first crucial step is often the hardest: defining your vision. Yet, it is this step that lays the foundation for everything else. Without vision, growth is aimless; with it, every challenge becomes purposeful, and that's where you want to be.

My vision started simple: cooking in the kitchen. Then it quickly became more. My mother and father had introduced me to cooking, and each had their own unique ways of preparing meals. But somewhere along the way, I realized that cooking was about more than just putting food on the table; it was a source of pure thrill and sparked so much curiosity in me I couldn't ignore it. I was fascinated with transforming ingredients into something delicious and comforting, and that feeling gripped me deeply. I didn't know exactly where this passion would lead, but I knew one thing: I had to chase it. Combine this fiery passion with a surge of impulsivity and restless energy, and you get a frenetic teenager—driven, but with a vision that kept the intensity burning. I am convinced my parents secretly wondered if there was a return policy on me back then.

So, at just fourteen years old, I was already feeling restless in the traditional school system. My heart was not in the classroom—I wanted to be in the kitchen, learning, creating, and experiencing the thrill of cooking. The idea of waiting any longer to pursue that dream felt impossible. Just three months later, my path became clear. I dropped out of traditional school and enrolled in a two-year apprenticeship in culinary arts. My mom, always supportive, even found me the perfect opportunity to immerse myself in this world I was so drawn to: a restaurant in my hometown, run by a chef she went to school with. It felt like everything was falling into place.

At the core of every meaningful change is a deliberate understanding of where you are headed. Vision is not just a distant dream; it is a carefully crafted map that outlines your purpose, ambitions, and the path you intend to take. Without a clear vision, it is easy to get lost in the noise of daily life, swayed by distractions or short-term goals that do not align with your true purpose. When you define your vision, you give yourself permission to imagine a future that excites and challenges you. Defining your vision ensures that the decisions you make and the steps you take, no matter how small, are moving you in the right direction.

But your vision must be authentic. It cannot be borrowed from someone else's idea of success. It must come from that spark of curiosity and genuine ambition. You are creating a future that aligns with who you truly are, not just what sounds good on paper. So be honest with yourself: What truly matters to you? Define that and let it guide everything you do. Start by creating a clear, vivid picture of the career you want to build, not a loose idea or vague hope for the future. If you do not have that picture just yet, then continue your search. I promise you are not behind. In fact, if you are reading this book and even thinking about your vision, you are already ahead of the game.

Paint a picture in your mind of a career that feels fulfilling, meaningful, and true to who you are. This picture is about more than material success or external achievements. It is about how you want to feel every day, the impact you want to have, and, most importantly, the relationships you want to cultivate. Forget the five-year plan for a second. Just give yourself ten quiet minutes each week to run the tape forward, imagine a regular day at work, but one where you are showing up as the leader you actually want to be. Not standing on a stage or winning awards, just handling the rush, leading a team, and solving a problem without losing your cool. What does that version of you sound like? How does that version of you hold yourself when someone drops the ball? What kind of energy do people feel when that future you walks into a room? Get specific. Then write down a moment or two that stands out from this exercise. Pick one thing—maybe the way you communicate, the way you set the tone, or the way you pause before reacting—and start practicing that thing in real life that same day. That is how change happens. Quietly, repeatedly, intentionally. And on your terms.

Track your progress monthly, not just the external results you see but the internal growth you feel, like how your confidence is building or how your mindset is shifting. Focus on whether your actions are helping you become that person you envision. But don't confuse your vision with a destination. Most people think of defining a vision solely in terms of the results they want to achieve and the titles they want to have. **However, the deeper, more transformative aspect of vision focuses on the person you must become in the process of realizing your vision.** If you focus solely on outcome, you will certainly miss the necessary internal growth and mindset shifts required to bring your vision to life. That is guaranteed.

Imagine you are a chef (or maybe you're already a chef), standing in front of an empty cooking pot, ready to craft something amazing and necessary. Into that pot, you pour your dreams, your ambitions, and your values, stirring them like ingredients in a recipe. These elements will blend into a single, powerful vision, gaining clarity and purpose, and the direction will become rich and full of flavors. This process will define not just what you want but why you want it. Having a vision transforms your curiosity into progress and clarifies the why behind your actions. When things get hard—and trust me, they will—that vision will keep you anchored.

I remember one night in Arles at L'Atelier de Jean Luc Rabanel: just minutes before service, the Chef walked in, glanced at the entire bread production I had spent hours on, and without saying much, tossed it all in the trash. Not good enough. We were opening the doors to guests, and I had to start over. I stepped into the back, fuming, pissed off, muttering every French curse I could think of under my breath. I could not believe it. Hours of work, tossed like garbage, and we were minutes from service. I needed a second to pace, swear, and get that rage out of my system before walking back in and getting the job done. After taking a breath, I pulled myself together, refocused, and trusted the process I had trained for. I did not let the moment define me; I let my response do that.

Your vision is not measured when everything goes right; it is tested when everything goes wrong.

Now that you have a clear vision, make every choice with intention. You are no longer just moving—you are moving *toward* something that matters, and that feeling is both fantastic and contagious. It will give you, and those around you, a palpable energy. Remember, your vision is the foundation that will fuel your relentless pursuit of growth. Once you have it, hold onto it fiercely. Everything else will fall into place.

1.3 FORWARD FOCUS WITH INTENTION

At the age of sixteen, I had just completed my first two years of apprenticeship and gotten my degree in culinary arts. It was an eye-opening experience, but I knew it was just the beginning of my culinary journey. There was a pivotal moment during those early years when I realized that my path lay within the Michelin-starred world, the realm of gastronomic excellence. I did not want to settle for ordinary; I wanted to create experiences, to cook food that changed the way people felt about a meal. I wanted to be part of the culinary elite, where artistry, precision, and passion come together on the plate.

But that clarity did not come overnight. It was born out of countless hours of reflection (which is completely fine and expected) and from asking myself what I truly wanted again and again. I needed to know if that vision was *the* vision. Was there any alternative? Would I be good enough? Would I be capable? What if I pursue my vision and don't like it? What if it's too difficult? This reflection happened in my head, as I was not the writing-things-down type of person at the time. But if you're someone who finds writing helpful, consider writing down your own answers to these questions.

My vision eventually became clear: I wanted to work in

kitchens where the expectation of excellence, discipline, and work ethic was just as strong if not stronger than the expectations for the food we served. Having a vision, though, was not nearly enough. A vision without a plan is just a dream, and I was determined to make mine a reality. So, my next step was creating a detailed plan, a roadmap that would guide me toward this objective. I knew I had to find or create the right environment that aligned with my vision. I didn't want just any job; I needed to find the right fit.

When I asked for recommendations for the best restaurant in the area that would fit my two-year bachelor degree in culinary arts and hospitality management, L'Auberge des Glazicks consistently came up; this place was renowned for its celebrated chef, Olivier Bellin. At the beginning of Olivier Bellin's tenure, L'Auberge des Glazicks was a family-run inn located in the small village of Plomodiern, Brittany, which is about eight miles away from Châteaulin. Chef Olivier Bellin took over the kitchen in 1998 with the vision of transforming it into a fine dining destination that would celebrate the flavors and ingredients of his native region while introducing modern culinary techniques. Initially, the restaurant was a humble third generation establishment owned by his mother, Marie-Noelle, serving traditional Breton fare. However, with Chef Olivier Bellin's experience working in prestigious kitchens under Joël Robuchon and Alain Senderens, he began to reshape the menu, elevating the local cuisine to a new level. After learning all this, I decided that L'Auberge des Glazicks was exactly where I belonged; I needed to be part of that journey. This was a defining moment where I made landing a job there my vision and my forward focus for the following few years.

Building a roadmap—your "forward focus with intention"— happens when your vision turns into a persistent and steady force; and now it's time to act. Do not start your roadmap with a blank piece of paper and merely write down a list of goals. That won't cut it. Instead, consider the outcome you're aiming for; what does success actually look like for you, in your world, on your terms? Once you have that image, visualize the road you will need to take to make that image a reality. What does the grind actually look like?

When I set my sights on working in two- and possibly three-Michelin-star kitchens, I didn't just write "become a great chef." I mapped out my moves; where I needed to train, which chefs I wanted to learn from, what sacrifices would come with my vision. I knew I would face long hours, possible rejection, and burnout. I knew I would have to prove myself over and over again. So I prepared for all of it. I studied menus in my downtime, I learned how to work stations I was not assigned to, and I made meals for the staff to get feedback. That is the level of clarity and intention I wanted for myself. Success does not come from simply writing down our goals. It comes from envisioning the process from the very beginning and sticking to it, especially when it starts to hurt.

Remember, your roadmap is your foundation, a deliberate

plan that ensures every action you take moves you closer to where you want to be. It turns your intentions into reality. When you approach your roadmap with this forward focus, you send a message to your friends, your family, and yourself: *I am not leaving my growth to chance.* Each decision, each step becomes a conscious move toward the person you are becoming.

Forward focus means knowing where you are headed, but it also means giving yourself the space to adjust, grow, and pivot if necessary. There is power in being both focused and flexible. Too often, people think a roadmap locks them into a certain path, but the reality is that it only locks out distractions and hesitations as you move toward what truly matters to you. It certainly does not mean you won't face challenges or need to adjust your course. You absolutely will, trust me. But with a roadmap, those challenges become part of the process, not roadblocks. Every detour you encounter will be a learning experience that builds your confidence instead of diminishing it. And here is where inspiration really begins. Once you start living your roadmap with forward focus, you will realize that real transformation happens on the way toward your vision—it happens because of the process itself. Each step forward brings you new growth and a deeper understanding of your own potential. Before you know it, you're not just following a roadmap, you're creating your future in real time.

As you build your roadmap and set your forward focus with intention, know that you are creating the strongest foundation possible for your journey ahead. But remember this: while a roadmap gives you clarity and purpose, it does not promise certainty. In fact, the further you travel down the path of growth, the more you will encounter moments where the unexpected unfolds and your plans no longer fit reality. When this happens, it's time to adjust.

1.4 THE VALUE OF THE UNEXPECTED

Even the best-laid plans will not account for everything. The path to growth is never a straight line, and while your roadmap gives you direction, it is the unexpected twists and turns that often provide the most profound opportunities for transformation. The journey deepens when you step into the unknown with confidence, when you embrace uncertainty as a crucial part of your growth, not as something to fear.

That is exactly what I had to do when I met Chef Olivier Bellin for the first time. It was a Saturday morning in spring, and the air carried a fresh maritime scent. I did not have my driver's license yet, so my father drove me to L'Auberge des Glazicks in the small village of Plomodiern. He was my ride, but the gravity of the day was all on me! I knew I had to prove myself, and I had to do it on my own. Chef Bellin, not yet awarded Michelin stars, had already made a name for himself with his bold approach to Breton cuisine. Our meeting was scheduled for 10 a.m., and I arrived exactly on time—punctual, as always. The restaurant's stone façade had an old-world charm to it, and as I stood there, taking it in, I felt a mix of excitement and nerves. This was my chance to work under one of Brittany's rising stars in the culinary world. That was my vision!

At 10 a.m., Chef Olivier himself opened the door. He was massive, with a presence that immediately filled the seemingly infinite space around him. His eyes went from me to my father, and then, with a mocking smile, he said, "Do you need your father to accompany you to the interview?" His words threw me for a moment.

I had not expected the conversation to begin this way, but after a brief pause, I smiled back and responded, "No, Chef. I am fine by myself." Little did he know that behind my confident answer I was trembling. My heart raced, my palms were sweating, and though I stood tall, I was suddenly overwhelmed by intimidation. This was no ordinary meeting—this was my shot at working in a kitchen I admired. I knew this was the moment to show him I could stand on my own, even if my nerves told a different story.

The interview was unexpectedly brief. Chef Olivier wasted no time, asking me direct questions about my motivation and reasons for wanting to join his team. He did not care at all for long explanations—he wanted conviction and was very impatient, like he had better things to do than being with me.

"Why do you want to be here?" he asked, his voice sharp but steady, as though he was weighing my words even before I spoke. I told him about my desire to push myself, to be part of something greater. I told him I had a vision, and he looked at me, completely uninterested. He studied me for a moment before cutting to the chase. "You will be working long hours, and you will not eat much," he said, with no hint of apology. "I will check your grades every month to make sure you are focused outside of the kitchen too. And you will follow my instructions religiously. Do you understand?" I nodded. "Say goodbye to your friends and family. You won't see them for a while. This will be your life."

There was no softening of his tone, no room for negotiation. It was a warning more than an interview—a glimpse into the intensity of what was to come. And then he hit me with the final blow. "By the way, I cannot take you on for another three months. You will need to find something else to do until then." It felt like a punch in the gut. Three months? After everything he had just laid out, the thought of waiting felt unbearable. And what about my vision? My roadmap? I had everything planned out, my mind set. I was fully committed to starting immediately.

In that moment, it all felt so unfair, and the casual indifference with which he delivered this news only made it more painful to bear. I nodded and thanked him, knowing that I had to find a temporary solution in the meantime of joining his team—there was no other option. I walked out of L'Auberge des Glazicks with a mixture of relief and disappointment. The weight of his words hung over me, but so did the clarity of what was ahead. I had been given a glimpse into the demands of his kitchen—both physically and mentally—and it was up to me to prove that I could handle it.

I shared every detail of my conversation with Chef Olivier when I got back in the car. In truth, it did not feel like a conversation at all. My father, having spent his entire career in the military, was not fazed by the chef's high demands or intense expectations. He simply looked at me and said something that has stayed with me my entire career: "What are two years of difficulties, adversities, and hardships compared to the rest of your life? Two years is nothing!" Classic Dad—the guy who thought running ten miles before breakfast was a great way to "warm up" for the day. Two years sounded like a walk in the park to him.

But it wasn't those two years that daunted me; it was the three months of uncertainty that made me question everything. Those months became a test, not just of my patience but of my commitment to the path I had chosen. I did not know what the future would hold, but instead of waiting for answers, I chose to dive in. I found a job at a small pastry and bakery shop where my father knew the owners. I started work thinking my time there would simply be a way to fill those three months. But those three months changed me. I learned the art of desserts, cakes, and breads, and I discovered a passion I didn't even realize I had. What felt like an obstacle became a turning point, an unexpected chapter that never would've happened if Chef Olivier had hired me immediately. Those three months were the beginning of something new in my career. It led to some of the most rewarding roles in my journey, all the way to Executive Pastry Chef. It taught me that growth so often comes from the paths we never plan for. Talk about the value of the unexpected!

When you embrace uncertainty, you start to see that growth doesn't just happen when everything goes according to plan—it thrives in the gaps where you must adapt, learn, and evolve in ways you never anticipated. Your roadmap points the way, but the unknown stretches your capacity to think, act, and grow beyond your comfort zone. As you move forward, it is essential to trust the process, even when it seems like your plan is unraveling. That uncertainty is not a sign of failure; it is a sign that you are in the right place—the place where breakthroughs happen. Your road-map gets you to the door, but it is the unknown that invites you to open it and step into the next phase of your journey.

With all these principles in mind, you have not just set the stage for your growth—you are building the mindset that will carry you forward. Now, you stand at the threshold of something more. You have sparked your curiosity and defined your vision, and you're ready to embrace both clarity and uncertainty alike. What comes next is the moment where all of your preparation meets opportunity, some known and some unknown. To embark on this journey of relentless growth, you must now fortify your mindset for the road ahead. Your journey is just beginning!

CHAPTER 2

PREPPING THE MIND: EMBARKING ON THE JOURNEY

The word "prepping" captures the essence of what it means to be in a constant state of readiness, a concept drawn from the world of chefs. As chefs, we are always prepping—not for one event but for whatever might come our way. Prepping is not just about following a recipe; it is about thinking ahead, being in tune with the unexpected, staying sharp, and continuously adapting to the inevitable curveballs that arise. Prepping means always having enough mise en place done for a specific dish—because the moment you do not, that's when everyone orders it and you run out halfway through the dinner rush. Good luck telling the chef!

Life does not always fit itself into our neat and tidy schedules. That is why we must prep for it, staying in a constant state of readiness, both mentally and emotionally, for whatever challenges or opportunities that might arise. This mindset, or rather this state of being, keeps us fluid and adaptable. Prepping ourselves for the unknown cultivates a resilience and mental flexibility that helps us face any challenge with confidence and intention, no matter what life throws our way.

2.1 THE STRENGTH OF YET

"Not yet" is a simple phrase, but its impact is profound. It reminds us that where we are now is not where we'll always be. When we say, "I cannot do this yet," we're acknowledging that growth takes time and that it will happen, no matter what. Take off the pressure. Unapologetically remind yourself that you do not need all the answers today. And, most importantly, give yourself permission to be in progress.

The mindset shift from "I can't" to "not yet" is a powerful game-changer in how we view self-reflection and acceptance. This small but significant reframe opens up so many possibilities to learn, to explore, and to develop—pivitol aspects of continued growth. The goal is no longer "to arrive" at success but to recognize and appreciate that growth is a lifelong journey.

In my first year as an apprentice at L'Auberge des Glazicks, every day felt like a pursuit of something bigger. We were driven by a singular goal: earning our first Michelin star. The intensity of that first year was far beyond anything I had imagined. We were not just in the pursuit of that Michelin star; we were surviving in the kitchen every single day. We were perpetually short-staffed, and it felt like there was never enough time to rest despite the restaurant being closed two days a week. It was hard to fully disconnect and recover because I knew what awaited us the next day. We spent countless hours in the kitchen, pushing through fatigue and exhaustion most of the time. There was no room for error and the pressure was immense, especially for me as an apprentice. I remember feeling the weight of each service, day after day, knowing that we were building something greater than just a meal—we were building our worth as a team. A team that was way too sparse, often with just Chef Olivier, me, and a sous-chef. And no dishwasher—the unsung hero of every culinary operation. (Whatever you do in your hospitality career, treat the dishwashers like royalty, or you will find yourself washing dishes after a twelve-hour day.)

At any given moment, a Michelin inspector could be seated in the dining room, silently evaluating every detail of our work. That knowledge kept us sharp, daily pushing for perfection, as we knew that four surprise visits over the course of a year would determine if we were ready for the accolade. Any lapse in focus could mean the difference between excellence and mediocrity. The smallest mistake—an overcooked piece of fish, a sauce slightly off, a texture meant to be crispy served soft or chewy, an ice cream too hard to make a "*quenelle*," even a lukewarm plate instead of piping hot one—could mean a setback...for another year. We had to execute everything with precision, driven by the dream of that star, and the majority of the time, it really felt like we were doing everything right.

It was during that time I learned the true meaning of dedication, and the lesson has stuck with me ever since, infusing itself into everything I do. It was not enough to be good; I had to be exceptional, day in and day out, with no guarantee that my efforts would be rewarded. I came to understand that I could mess something up in the same amount of time it took to get it right, so why not just apply myself from the get-go.

When the Michelin guide was finally released that year, and we didn't receive the star, it was profoundly devastating. After an entire year of dedication, striving for consistency and flawless execution, I started to question everything: *How is this possible? I asked myself. What more could I have done? How can I possibly do better than this past year? How much did I contribute to missing the common goal?* The disappointment was heavy because I didn't quite know how we missed the mark. Yet, it was in that very moment when the defeat sunk in that I understood the power of "not yet."

Although we hadn't reached our goal, the journey wasn't over. "Not yet" became a vital lesson. Instead of allowing failure to define me and the team, it became the fuel we needed to keep going. The pursuit of that star was not over—it was only delayed.

The very next day, Chef Olivier gathered the team. I walked in with my head low, my stomach tight, fully expecting a harsh debrief. I was bracing myself for disappointment, maybe even blame; part of me was sure he would single me out. The silence in the room was heavy. We had poured everything into that year, hoping for the Michelin star, and we'd come up short. Then Chef looked around at all of us, calm, collected, and simply said, "It is OK, we were not ready yet."

That was it. No yelling, no speeches, no breakdown of what went wrong. Just those words. And somehow they cut deeper than anything else. Because in that moment, I realized he was not defeated; he was already looking forward. He wasn't dismissing our effort; his words were a quiet challenge to evolve. His restraint spoke volumes. He was the one most affected, the one who had every reason to be upset, but there he was, standing with us, encouraging the team. He acknowledged the tremendous effort we had put in over the past year and showed true appreciation. "It is time now to refocus, refine, elevate and push ourselves further," he concluded. And with that, we went on like nothing ever happened.

Consistency at that level of execution is one of the hardest things to achieve, but the belief that our time is coming, just "not yet," is a step toward greatness that carries us forward. It is a reminder that the journey, with all its pressure and intensity, is part of what makes success so meaningful when it finally comes. Growth is always incremental. The most fulfilled, successful people in any field did not achieve that greatness overnight.

The most profound growth happens in the space between

where you are now and where you are headed. You are not fixed; you are constantly developing, and you are no longer bound by limitations but motivated by what is to come. While you fuel your growth with the strength of "not yet," it is imperative that you keep yourself aligned with your values by staying true to who you are. But in order to know who you are, you must move forward with purpose and self-awareness.

2.2 NAVIGATING THE MIND MIRROR

What stories do you tell yourself about your abilities? Where are you most afraid of failing? Do you see intelligence, skill, and talent as fixed traits, or do you believe you can cultivate them over time? Your answers to these questions are critical because they will uncover the mental blocks preventing you from moving toward your vision. You must reflect deeply on your current beliefs because it is almost impossible to chart a path forward without understanding your strengths, weaknesses, and values.

But first thing first, you must know where you stand. Having a deep, honest relationship with yourself means knowing what drives you, what holds you back, and how you react to different situations. Without this self-awareness, your journey will lack direction because you won't know what to work on.

I vividly remember the very beginning of my second year of apprenticeship at L'Auberge des Glazicks. We were finally getting some traction with hiring staff. Although they didn't necessarily stay long, I was thrilled about getting some much-needed support, even if just for a week at the time. It seemed as if many of them thought that working in a Michelin star restaurant was some type of survival training! I remember watching some cooks who had been in the industry much longer than me or had come from reputable restaurants in Paris, a Michelin-star hub at the time. Their precision was always on point, but I could sense a difference between those who were fulfilled in their work and those who were merely enduring it. I could see it in their eyes—some were pushing themselves more, driven by their own relentless pursuit of growth, while others were just going through the motions. I wondered if they could see those things in themselves, which made me wonder what I might be missing in my own approach. It was that year I decided self-awareness would be my guide. I couldn't accept the idea of burning out before I got to truly begin. That future was unsettling, and avoidable.

I started by carving out just ten to fifteen minutes a day for self-reflection, usually after service when the kitchen was finally quiet. I would sit in the back with something to snack on, usually something sweet as I have a sweet tooth, and go over the day in my head. Not the dishes or the numbers, but me. How did I show up? Did I lose my patience? Did I lead the way I wanted to lead? Sometimes I would scribble a few lines on the back of my prep list for the next day or on an old ticket from service. It was not a polished process, but it was real. And after a while, those short check-ins started to show me my truth: where I was slipping, where I was growing, and what kind of leader I was becoming. That is where self-awareness starts—in the quiet, after the heat, when you are willing to take an honest look at yourself.

However you decide to approach this self-reflection, do not cancel on yourself, even if it's tempting. Choose a place where you feel relaxed, inspired, and free from distractions. For me, this place has changed many times depending on where I lived, but my all-time favorite spot was on Kauai's North Shore in Hawaii. I worked within walking distance of my apartment, and every day I would sit on a bench overlooking Hanalei Bay and reflect. Most of the time, this happened after the night shift, under the clear sky and bright moon, the waves crashing against the nearby cliffs. I easily spent an hour there each time—who was I to complain about showing up for self-reflection with a view like that?

The next step toward self-awareness is mindfully choosing something to reflect on. If you've never reflected before, though, just sit alone and let your mind wander. That's totally fine too; let it come naturally—I promise you it will.

By taking the time to reflect, you will realize that the key to lasting fulfillment is not just about mastering techniques or earning accolades, it's about embracing a mindset that pushes you beyond your comfort zone. Fulfillment won't come from hard work alone; it comes from consistently asking yourself why you are working so hard and where it is leading you. Self-awareness will give you a clear picture of where you're at and where you're headed. It will serve as your internal compass, helping you recognize where you're growing and where you're spinning in circles. This "mind mirror," as I call it, is a reflective tool that allows you to observe your thoughts, beliefs, and emotions with clarity, guiding you toward self-awareness, personal, and professional growth. But as you embark on this journey, it's extremely important to recognize what is happening in your mind without judgment. Let me repeat that: view your current thoughts and beliefs without any kind of judgment. Be kind to yourself!

Often, the reflection you see in your "mind mirror" is shaped by past experiences, old fears, and inherited beliefs that no longer serve you. Question the reflections that have held you back until now. Are they truly yours or are they the result of external influences? Do they represent your current reality or are they distorted images of who you used to be? **Self-awareness will help you differentiate between what is real and what is simply a projection of outdated beliefs and fears.**

During my early years, I was driven by one core fear: that if I ever stopped pushing, ever slowed down or admitted I didn't know something, I would fall behind or, worse, be replaced. I tied my worth to performance, perfection, and this crazy need to prove myself. I remember one night in particular, working insane hours at L'Auberge Des Glazicks. I had not slept properly in days, and the pressure to be "on" was crushing. I found myself standing in the walk-in cooler, heart pounding, eyes burning, whispering to myself that I could not keep doing this; then I walked out pretending everything was fine. That fear of being seen as anything less than invincible had me trapped. It was not until I broke down days later in a quiet moment alone that I realized the fear was not real—it was a story I had told myself all this time. And that story was costing me peace, presence, and purpose. Letting it go was not easy, but it was necessary. It took me several years to get a grasp on that fear and not let it continue trapping me. That is what self-awareness can do: it doesn't just show you where you are, it frees you from who you no longer need to be.

The more you engage in reflection, the clearer your self-awareness becomes. Staring into your "mind mirror" is far from a waste of time; this practice teaches you to pause and examine your thoughts with curiosity instead of criticism. Your image is not fixed; it is fluid and capable of changing as you change and grow.

Just to be clear, self-reflection is not about fixing what is "wrong" with you. It is simply about understanding who you are, as you are, so you can finally free yourself from external expectations and unconscious habits. And you alone get to decide how you want to show up in the world from now on.

Do you believe you're limited by who you have always been, or do you dare to imagine who you could be? This question is where a fixed mindset and a growth mindset collide. A fixed mindset keeps you stuck thinking, *This is just the way I am.* That thought may feel familiar to you. But a growth mindset tells you that transformation is limitless, that you can become more than the person you see in this moment. The reflection staring back at you is not your final form. It is an invitation to grow into the person you envision.

2.3 FROM LIMITATION TO POSSIBILITY

Shifting from a fixed mindset to a growth mindset is one of the hardest transitions someone can make, and it is not as simple as flipping a switch. I am still actively working on that transition in some aspects of my life, so believe me when I say it is very hard. It entails rebuilding the foundations of how you have always understood yourself, your potential, and the world around you.

When you have a fixed mindset, you are often locked in by fear—fear of failing, fear of being judged, or even fear of your own potential. Shifting into a growth mindset forces you to confront the fear of appearing weak or wrong, threatening to destroy your ego and pride as you go against everything you once believed was the right path. It feels like rewriting your identity, and somewhere along the way, you cannot help but wonder who you really are as you are forced to let go of the person you thought you always had to be. With a fixed mindset, you might feel like your abilities are cemented, as if you have reached your limit, and that becomes your comfort zone. Leaving that zone feels like stepping into complete uncertainty, and let's be honest—it is terrifying.

The journey of shifting into a growth mindset is filled with doubt; it is both messy and uncomfortable. You will not see results every day, and that is the hardest part. You are constantly questioning if you're making any progress, wondering if it's even worth it or if you'll just end up where you started. The idea of embracing challenges rather than running from them is not something that feels natural at first. You have probably spent years if not decades thinking that success should come easily, and when it doesn't, it feels like a personal failure. But here's the thing: no one talks about how often you must fight your own instincts on this path. Every step back feels personal. Every time you do not see immediate progress or feel pressured by results, that little voice in the back of your head tells you to give up, that you are not capable of change. Overcoming that voice is not about silencing it. It is about learning to keep moving despite it.

The shift from a fixed mindset to a growth mindset is the cornerstone of self-improvement. So, how do you recognize it? A fixed mindset tells you that your abilities are static, that no matter how much effort you put in, you will always be limited by your inherent traits. This belief impedes growth. It keeps you from trying new things because you are afraid of failing. It traps you in a cycle of self-doubt, where challenges become threats to your identity rather than opportunities to grow. A growth mindset, on the other hand, tells you that your abilities can be developed through effort, learning, and, most importantly, perseverance. This outlook opens up new possibilities because it diminishes the fear of failure. Instead of being paralyzed by the thought of making mistakes, you become energized by the chance to learn from them.

My second year of apprenticeship at L'Auberge des Glazicks was even more demanding. The reality hit hard: our best, up to that point, was not enough to receive that first Michelin star. But Chef Olivier, in his quiet, unshakable way, refused to let us dwell on the loss. Instead, he challenged us to look deeper, to ask ourselves the uncomfortable questions. Where did we fall short? What could we do better? These moments of reflection were grueling—full of extreme self-scrutiny—and they were necessary. We could not keep doing the same thing and expecting a different outcome. He demanded more from everyone, including himself, and he was determined to lead the way. There was no room for error.

The energy in the kitchen shifted. We had to adopt a new way of thinking: complacency was our greatest enemy, and complacency had no business among us. We had to grow, we had to shift, we had to stop pushing for minor improvements and rethink everything—it was our only option. We pushed ourselves to levels we did not know we could reach. Every day, I felt the pressure, I was exhausted, but I never said any of that out loud. I wasn't the type of person to give anyone or anything the satisfaction of knowing that such a relentless grind could break me, but, man, I felt it. Perfection was not an option; it was a requirement, an obligatory condition. The stakes were too high.

We had no idea when the Michelin inspector would return, but we could not afford to wait until we knew. With his voice calm and firm, Chef Olivier would remind us daily, "We need to be ready at any moment." Service after service, we pushed our limits. Exhaustion became part of our routine, but so did our belief in what we were creating. "If you are not pushing harder today than yesterday, then you are failing the entire team," Chef Olivier would say. We never settled; we questioned ourselves constantly about how we could improve and we went nonstop because, "Good enough will never be good enough for people like us," he would often say.

Those were the longest 365 days of my life—an entire year of intensity and refinement. We didn't know if our efforts would even pay off. The wait for the Michelin guide was excruciating, so we worked with an air of uncertainty over us. What if the select few days in the year when we were not on our A-game was the very day the Michelin inspector paid us a visit? What if we scored perfectly from a food quality standpoint but, on that specific day, the front of the house did not perform their best? I could only control so much, especially as an apprentice. The rest was up to our ability as a team.

Then, one day, the news came: we had finally earned the first star. A rush of emotions followed that I cannot fully describe to this day. It was intense, as though each effort we made came flooding back in one singular, glorious moment. The relief was overwhelming too, knowing that everything we had done, all the late nights and sacrifices, had been worth it. It was one of the best feelings I've experienced in my career, that sense of validation and triumph rushing through me all at once. That unforgettable moment has stayed with me ever since because it wasn't just about finally getting the star, it was about the journey it took to get there, the transformation we had undergone as individuals and as a team. That star was the direct result of the growth mindset Chef Olivier instilled in us. It was proof that when you push beyond your limits, question everything, and embrace the process of constant improvement, achieving something close to greatness becomes possible. Over the course of those two years, I had adopted the process and now had a deep understanding of a growth mindset, so the star represented far more than recognition; it was a moment of victory I would never forget.

To successfully shift from a fixed mindset to a growth mindset—from limitation to possibility—it is essential to not only embrace your belief that abilities can be developed but to also build the endurance required to sustain that growth over time. Your mental flexibility is the key to maintaining this endurance, allowing you to adapt and persevere throughout the journey.

2.4 ENDURING GROWTH, BENDING MINDS

So far, we have only scratched the surface of the growth journey, and that's what makes this next part so exciting. Until now, we have simply laid the groundwork necessary to embark on this path—the real work is ahead, and it's about to get far more interesting. Your mind must be ready to bend, adapt, and endure in order to fully embrace your transformation.

As we delve deeper into the concepts of endurance and mental flexibility, it is important to remember the foundational principles that guide this journey: enduring patience, resilience in the face of adversities, perseverance through failures, adaptability in the midst of change, and progress over perfection. This section provides a high-level introduction to the core principles of perseverance and adaptability—key drivers of long-term growth, professional evolution, and resilience in the face of uncertainty. It sets the stage for the mindset you'll need to build mental endurance.

As many have said before me: "Success is a marathon, not a sprint." Endurance is not just the ability to withstand pressure, it is the ability to stay committed to your growth, even when the path becomes uncertain. It is the mental stamina that keeps you moving forward. But here's the truth: real endurance requires flexibility. If you stick rigidly to one plan, pushing yourself simply for the sake of sticking to that plan, you will burn out. Believe me, I have done this countless times in my early years, all while hoping for different results. I was so locked into the idea of becoming a Michelin-starred chef that I convinced myself every sacrifice was part of the path. I did not think I was losing myself; I thought I was defining who I was. Every sleepless night, every move, every moment of pressure felt like fuel. Insanity, you would say, right? Endurance, in its most powerful form, is about adapting to change while maintaining your focus and purpose, not about running out of fuel because you've burned through it all to achieve a singular destination or goal.

Getting that first star at L'Auberge des Glazicks was a true test of my endurance. I foolishly believed that pushing myself to the limit, no matter the cost, was the key to success. I was operating on very little sleep, day in and day out, hoping that my hard work and dedication would eventually pay off. It took a pretty bad car accident several months after my eighteenth birthday to change how I worked. I was shaken so deeply that I knew I had to make a change in how I approached my life and my goals.

Before the accident, my mindset was fixed, and I thought willpower would be enough to break through anything in my way. I was utterly convinced that if I just pushed harder, stayed longer, and outworked everyone I would eventually get there. But I kept hitting the same wall. It was not until I started embracing flexibility that I truly understood what endurance meant—and it was not about grinding myself into the ground as I'd thought. I realized I had to adapt, to bend without breaking if I wanted to achieve long-term growth. That meant checking in with myself regularly and letting go of the belief that there was only one "right" way to succeed. I started adjusting my approach mid-service instead of forcing a system that wasn't working. I paid attention to what the moment actually called for, not just what I had planned. That is when things started to shift from surviving the pressure to thriving in it.

Flexibility matters at every stage of growth, as you will encounter setbacks, obstacles, and unexpected turns throughout life, especially with a career in hospitality. Hospitality is unpredictable, and no plan goes as perfectly as intended. Flexibility enables you to pivot in these moments without losing momentum. Sometimes you will need to adjust your strategy and realign your goals in order to keep moving forward with renewed energy. Flexibility also does not mean abandoning your vision or "forward focus"; it means finding different ways to achieve it. You must shift course, when necessary, but never lose sight of where you are going.

Remember: growth does not happen on a set timeline. Sometimes progress is slower than we would like. There will be moments on the journey when it feels like you are taking one step forward and two steps back. For seasoned leaders, this is especially critical. You have seen cycles of growth, setbacks, and recovery. You understand that success rarely follows a straight line. But in the face of setbacks, it is easy to become rigid, to stick to what worked in the past because, well, it worked in the past, so why not try that same thing again? But we also become locked into our path because that's what feels safe. It's familiar. It's something we know when everything else is falling away.

Endurance will prepare you for difficult times, and there will be many of them, but endurance is about more than surviving through these hard times—it is about thriving through them. Think of it like this: a rigid tree might break in a storm, but a flexible one bends and sways with the wind, enduring the storm while remaining rooted. For both new professionals and seasoned leaders, cultivating endurance through bending and adapting your mind is a lifelong practice, not a one-time effort.

The growth you experience in the early stages of your journey won't look the same as it will years later, but the principles remain the same: flexibility leads to greater endurance, and true endurance requires flexibility. For those of you in leadership roles already, you are not just responsible for your own growth, you are leading teams, projects, and entire divisions or businesses. How you handle setbacks will set the tone of those who follow you. I guarantee you that your ability to lead with endurance and flexibility will inspire those around you to do the same.

To the next generation of leaders, embracing flexibility means understanding that success and career fulfillment will not always be immediate. Growth takes time, and your path will not always be linear. The true essence of enduring growth lies not just in overcoming the obstacles that come your way but in embracing those obstacles as part of your process. Your ability to bend without breaking is what defines true growth. That flexible yet determined mindset will keep you rooted, resilient, and constantly evolving. The journey is ongoing, but with endurance and flexibility, you will be ready for whatever comes next.

CHAPTER 3

SEASONING YOUR AMBITION: ENDURING PATIENCE

Today, the idea of waiting seems almost outdated. We're living in a world where everything is at our fingertips. Since the rise of technology and digital platforms has drastically altered our daily lives, the concept of patience seems antiquated. People like you and me have gotten used to getting what we want with the click of a button: instant messaging, streaming entertainment on demand, food delivered in under an hour, even groceries or consumer goods arriving within a day. Social media apps flood us with dopamine hits through likes, comments, and endless scrolling. Every second, new content is posted to captivate and hold our attention. And it works! I am certainly guilty as charged.

Instant gratification is deeply rooted in these innovations, and waiting—even for a moment—has become an extraordinarily uncomfortable experience. Despite these conveniences, the pace of meaningful growth has not changed; there are no shortcuts to developing true expertise, building mental resilience, and fostering authentic self-development. So, let's cut to the chase and confront some hard truths.

Many young professionals enter the workforce today expecting fast promotions and immediate recognition, and they quickly face burnout, frustration, and disappointment when they don't see results that align with those expectations. Studies show that this generation, particularly Gen Z, reports higher levels of stress than previous generations, partly due to this desire for quick success and the unrealistic standards set by social media and influencer culture.[1] In the US, one out of three Gen Zs and one out of four millennials have reported their mental health as poor or extremely poor. More than nine in ten Gen Zs between the ages of eighteen and twenty-one say they have experienced at least one physical or emotional symptom due to stress in the past month. Constant exposure to curated images of success and achievement creates both unrealistic expectations and a sense of competition. It is linked directly to increased levels of anxiety and lower self-esteem. In contrast, professionals who develop their skills over time, consistently work through challenges, and build

---

[1] Erica Coe, Andrew Doy, Kana Enomoto, and Cheryl Healy, "Gen Z mental health: The impact of tech and social media," McKinsey Health Institute, April 28, 2023, https://www.mckinsey.com/mhi/our-insights/gen-z-mental-health-the-impact-of-tech-and-social-media.

strong foundations tend to find more lasting success and overall satisfaction than those who expect fast results.

In the most recent years of my career in the hospitality industry, I've observed a growing trend that presents a big challenge to the evolution of leadership and the preservation of a values-driven hospitality culture. The word "entitled" has been thrown around too many times to describe the current generation of leaders and younger professionals. But I strongly believe what we're witnessing play out in our kitchens and workplaces is not so much an issue of entitlement but a disconnect in our understanding of the pathway to leadership. For example, I have witnessed younger professionals step in to cover a few shifts for their direct supervisor, and, after doing so, they suddenly expect more—a considerable raise, an immediate promotion, or a significant boost in responsibility. For whatever reason, they associate those markers with "success" in today's society. While I recognize the value in taking initiative, this momentary experience of covering a supervisor's shift does not equate to the depth required for shouldering a full-time leadership role. Leadership demands continuous learning, problem-solving, and the ability to make decisions that impact the entire team—skills that take more time and intention to develop than simply covering a few shifts. Leadership requires a huge amount of patience and foresight that only comes from consistently putting in hard work over time.

Couple this challenge with another: when current leaders, including myself more than a few times, fail to properly mentor and guide these individuals after they step up, we end up cocreating the belief that external markers of success will (or should) follow. If a leader's feedback is poorly delivered or unclear (and it often is), their reports experience feelings of disappointment, a sense that they were not given a proper chance, or, in worstcase scenarios, complete disengagement. This can happen in a matter of a few days, and when it does, it's not just the young professional who struggles; the leader must now navigate these feelings and the consequences of their own miscommunication. Often, these leaders are not properly equipped with the adequate skills to manage this situation, and that's not their fault. They were probably not mentored or coached either, instead expected to *just know* and *just fix it.*

This all-too-common scenario is not about pointing fingers at our current leaders or about name-calling our young professionals "entitled." It is about recognizing that, without proper coaching and mentorship, we risk losing those with the most potential in the future of our industry. It is our job now to show that leadership involves more than temporary responsibility; earning a leadership role requires consistent effort, growth, endurance, and patience. But there are leaders who are capable of this and leaders who aren't.

Throughout my career, I have learned to assess mentors by watching how they handle pressure, how they speak to others when they think no one else is listening, and how they invest, or don't invest, in people. Some leaders just extract results and care little for those who make those results possible. If you are consistently confused, overlooked, or shrinking under someone's leadership, that is your signal—they are not an adequate mentor. A good mentor makes you feel stretched, not small. And when that stretch turns into silence or doubt, it is time to reassess and possibly move on.

3.1 DODGING THE SHORTCUT TRAP

After completing my apprenticeship at L'Auberge des Glazicks, I stayed on for the summer season to help the team. It felt good to support a kitchen I had grown with, but deep down, I knew my time there was coming to an end. After two years of relentless work and achieving Michelin-star status, I was ready for the next big step. My sights were set on working at one of the best 2 Michelin star restaurants in Brittany. L'Amphitryon, under the leadership of Chef Jean-Paul Abadie, felt like a leap that would take me from where I was to where I wanted to be. I was starting to fill with excitement and anticipation for this new chapter.

But then life threw me another curveball. The restaurant I had my eyes on could not take me until the following spring season, which meant seven months of waiting for my vision to become reality. I was again at a crossroads. I had worked tirelessly for two years, and now all I needed to take my next step forward was to wait just a little longer. But waiting was unbearable. My impatience began to consume me, and that is when I fell into what I now call the "shortcut trap."

Instead of seeing the wait as an opportunity to refine my skills or strengthen my abilities, I let my emotions take control. My impatience morphed into stubbornness, and that stubbornness clouded my judgment. You would think by then I would have learned, but as it turned out, I was still as stubborn as a souffle that refuses to rise.

I could not wait seven months. I had convinced myself that moving forward meant moving *now*. I was not thinking clearly; I just wanted out. And so, without much thought, I made the decision to leave L'Auberge des Glazicks, walking away from the restaurant and the team that had shaped me over the past two years. I left with no job lined up, no real plan—just a burning desire to move forward, whatever that meant at the time. But in my rush, I did not realize I was actually moving sideways.

After weeks of procrastination, the reality of my situation hit me hard. I was directionless, with no clear path in sight. The excitement of leaving had faded, and I found myself stuck in limbo. So, I decided I needed to do something, *anything*. I turned my attention to Courchevel, in the Savoie region, a place that promised seasonal work for winter and the possibility of something fresh. It was not part of my original plan, but at least it was a direction.

I applied to several Michelin star restaurants in Courchevel, hoping to salvage my Michelin dream, but I had waited too long.

I was too late in the hiring process. Most teams were already full, and the opportunities I had hoped for were, unfortunately, no longer available. One chef, after a brief phone call, said bluntly, "We needed someone two weeks ago. Where were you?" Another didn't even respond. And so, I settled for an Italian restaurant called La Cendrée, in the center of the village. Settling…just saying the word felt like failure. Working there was not something I had envisioned for myself, not after the years of discipline and sacrifice. But there I was, in a kitchen I had not dreamed of, serving cuisine I had not trained for. It was humbling. And it was the reality I had created through my own impatience. But there is a lesson in that—one I didn't fully understand at the time.

I realized then how much I needed to learn the value of patience. My eagerness to move forward, to take the next step, blinded me to the importance of waiting for the *right* opportunity. I was so focused on the idea of progress that I forgot to trust the process. It was a hard lesson, one that I had to learn firsthand, but it profoundly changed my perspective. After that experience, I made a promise to myself: from that point on, I would take the time to self-reflect before making any major decisions in my career. The question I came up with then and continue to ask myself to this day is, "Is this opportunity the next logical step for the following opportunity after that?" I realized that ambition, while critical, needed to be tempered with patience. I had to season my ambition, let it mature instead of rushing toward the next big thing. Self-development, I realized, was not just about moving forward; it was about making sure each step aligned with where I truly wanted to go.

I came to understand that patience is more than just waiting—I needed to trust that the right path would reveal itself if I was willing to give it time. I needed to slow down, to trust that by holding steady, I could still achieve my goals without compromising on my "forward focus." And that's exactly what I did from then on. That experience shaped me into the professional I am today—someone who still strives for greatness but now with the patience to let the journey unfold in its own time.

In a world where everything moves at lightning speed, it is easy to believe there's always a faster way to get to the top. The temptation to avoid the path you envisioned is everywhere. You might even feel that cutting a corner here or there will speed up your success. And that may be true—there is nothing stopping you from taking shortcuts. But here is the truth: Every shortcut comes with a consequence. When you try to fast-track your journey, you eventually must come back and do the work you tried to skip. It may not happen right away, but somewhere down the line, the gaps will become clear. This is especially true when you're making your way toward a promotion. You will realize that the very things you tried to avoid were actually key to your growth and now expected out of your performance. The lessons you bypass will come back to test you, and, more often than not, you will have to double back and fill in those gaps.

Patience is often seen as passive action, but it is anything but that. Patience is actively choosing to embrace the journey, to recognize that each step has value. The process itself—the learning, the challenges, the failures—is what prepares you for what lies ahead. As I said, if you are tempted to expedite your journey, there will be a price to pay, a repercussion to face. Whether it is a lack of readiness, missing key experiences, or not developing the resilience needed to handle future challenges, the price is always higher than the reward. When you dodge the shortcut trap, however, you give yourself time to grow into your role and develop skills that will serve you in the long run. You must be playing the long game, understanding that real, meaningful success and fulfillment is built over time, not overnight. And patience is what allows you to fully develop your potential. It is not a delay in progress; it is the space you need to grow in the right way, even if that means waiting for months that feel like years.

But patience and ambition require the delicate balance of knowing when to hold back and trust the process and when to let that drive, that fire, work for you rather than against you.

3.2 CHANNELING THE FIRE WITHIN

From the earliest stages of my career, I have felt the uncontainable force of ambition inside me, constantly urging me to go further, to reach higher. Anyone who knows me well will tell you this. Internally, I need to feel like I'm progressing, that each step is a meaningful climb toward becoming more than who I was before—not for the recognition that might bring but for the challenge itself. The higher I aim, the more I realize how essential ambition is, not only for me but for anyone serious about their personal and professional growth.

The boldness of my ambition has always made it hard to contain—it pushes against my boundaries, both external and internal. Most of the time, this drive felt overwhelming, and I had to learn to channel it, to contain it. But I believe that's what made it so powerful and important. The bolder my ambition, the harder it is to keep in check, which is exactly why the growth that comes from it is so rewarding. It is in those moments of striving for something beyond reach that true progress happens. I am utterly convinced that without this relentless pursuit, growth remains somewhat superficial. But in the willingness to embrace that uncontainable ambition, to push through the inevitable challenges, growth is both consequential and lasting.

For me, ambition is not just a desire to achieve—it is a moral responsibility to myself to never settle, to always keep learning, and to adopt the process of becoming better every single day. The higher the mountain, the more I understand that growth happens during the climb, and that the climb itself is fueled by the fire of ambition that I cannot and will not extinguish. Ambition is like a pristine ingredient waiting to be part of an unforgettable dish. I compare it to *Fleur de sel*, a type of sea salt hand harvested from the coast of Brittany, France, which retains its natural minerals and delicate flavor. It is considered one of the finest finishing salts in the world and sworn by chefs globally. In its raw form, ambition holds immense potential, but it is only when you learn to use its "seasoning" correctly that it transforms the unremarkable into something unforgettable. Just as a great chef does not overwhelm a dish with seasoning but instead uses experience to balance and elevate the natural flavor, ambition, too, must be fine-tuned, adding just the right amount at the right time to create the result you envision.

Working at the Italian restaurant felt like a daily battle with my ambition. It was not the workload or the expectations that made it hard—it was the overwhelming sense that I did not belong there. Courchevel, nestled in the French Alps, was a world-renowned ski resort village in Savoie, famous for its luxury, stunning mountain views, and premier skiing. Part of Les Trois Vallees, it offered high-end chalets and fine dining, attracting celebrities and winter sports enthusiasts alike.

La Cendrée restaurant felt like a hidden gem tucked away in the heart of this luxurious alpine village. From the moment you stepped inside, the cozy atmosphere wrapped around you like a warm embrace, especially on those very cold winter nights at 5,700 feet above sea level, when the snow blanketed the town. The restaurant had a rustic charm, its wood-paneled walls covered with pictures of the owner with guests who had visited over the decades, from celebrities to professional athletes to worldwide political figures. There was a sense of elegant homeliness to it. The fireplace from the wood pizza oven crackled in the corner, casting a gentle glow that added to its inviting ambience. The menu was a celebration of authentic Italian cuisine, a surprising find in the French Alps but a perfect match for the setting. The menu featured both authenticity and simplicity that spoke to the heart of Italian cooking, as the owners and the Executive Chef were all Italian. The pasta was handmade daily. (In fact, for a few months after my time there, my hands were rolling dough even in my sleep!) All our sauces simmered for hours, and the seafood was fresh from the Mediterranean Sea. There was a huge emphasis on quality, from the black-truffle-topped risottos tableside to the tender veal Milanese, all prepared with the precision and passion of the Italian chef in the kitchen.

My all-time favorite dish was the *Tagliolini con Tartufo Bianco d'Alba*, or Tagliolini with white truffle from Alba, Italy. It was an expensive indulgence but an exquisite one. We prepared the dish in the kitchen, but the real magic happened at the tableside. We brought out a cart with an entire wheel of *Parmigiano Reggiano*, weighing about eighty-five pounds and carved out from the top. The pasta, coated in a delicate cream sauce, was poured into the wheel, and stirred until the cheese melted, creating a luxurious, rich velvety texture to die for. Then the dish was plated and finished with freshly shaved white truffle from Alba—which could cost up to $650 for just 3.5 ounces—the epitome of expensive indulgence.

Despite this decadence and dreamy ambience, I remember waking up every morning with this voice in my head telling me I was wasting time, that I could be doing something more aligned with my goals. It wasn't just impatience; this voice signaled a deep internal conflict between where I was and where I wanted, or maybe needed, to be. But walking away was not an option. I had made a commitment, not just to the restaurant but to myself. Quitting would have been the easy way out, but I knew that if I left, I would be taking another shortcut that could rob me of something important. What was that "something"? I didn't know at the time, but I had to believe there was a lesson.

Patience became the hardest thing to practice while I was there because I was not used to waiting; I was used to pushing forward, fast. The days blurred into weeks, and every shift felt like a test of endurance, not physically but mentally. I had to learn to quiet that voice telling me to give up, and instead ask myself, "What can I learn from this?" Maybe I wasn't at the most prestigious restaurant, and maybe I wasn't where I thought I needed to be, but there was value in being uncomfortable; I had to believe that. That belief forced me to reflect, to understand that every experience, no matter how misaligned it feels in the moment, has a purpose. I needed to extract every bit of growth I could, even in a place that did not feel like "home." And, most importantly, I needed to keep my word to myself and show some integrity.

In the end, my time there was not just another job. I believe it was a test—a test of my commitment to my own growth, a reminder that sometimes the real challenge is not in the work itself but in managing my mindset when things don't go as planned.

I learned that ambition does not always mean moving forward as fast as possible; it also means knowing when to stay put and engaged wherever I am, holding on to the fact that growth comes from patience and staying the course. And, as a bonus, I did walk away with something tangible: I learned how to cook crazy good Italian cuisine. Being the only French chef in a kitchen full of Italians, I had the chance to absorb their techniques and flavors, learning firsthand what it takes to create authentic Italian dishes. That experience shaped me more than I realized at the time. I grew not just as a chef but as a person. I learned the true value of ambition is not just in the pursuit of progress but in the patience and endurance it demands along the way.

Growth requires both ambition to push forward and patience to guide the way. True progress is a delicate dance between these two forces. Ambition fuels your drive, and patience ensures that each step is intentional, building toward something lasting and meaningful. Said another way: **ambition drives the dream, but patience shapes its reality.**

3.3 THE SUBTLE DANCE OF DUAL FORCES

So, how do we get two opposites to complete each other? We need both in our pursuit of growth, but at first glance, patience and ambition seem to exist on opposite ends of the spectrum. Ambition pushes forward, fuels your hunger to achieve, and makes you restless for what's next. Patience, on the other hand, teaches you to embrace the present, to wait with grace, and to trust the process. Yet, despite their contrasting natures, these two forces are not in conflict—they complement each other beautifully, forming a partnership that is essential for career success and professional fulfillment.

Ambition without patience can certainly lead to recklessness. It can drive you to act too quickly, often without thinking things through, which can then lead to burnout, frustration, or costly mistakes if they involve a team or a division you're responsible for. In the hospitality industry, for example, I have seen young professionals so eager to climb the ladder that they leap at every opportunity, only to find themselves overwhelmed by the responsibility they have prematurely taken on. Their ambition was undeniable, even commendable for some, but without patience to guide and clarify their efforts, they ended up sacrificing long-term growth for short-term gains.

This scenario is more common than you might think—and it's easy to fall prey to, especially earlier in our careers. When navigating career transitions, timing and readiness matter just as much as drive. Before saying yes to the next title or promotion, ask yourself: Do I fully understand the expectations of this role? Have I mastered the level I'm at now? Do I have a mentor or support system to help me grow into this next phase? Saying no to the wrong move can sometimes be the most strategic decision you make. Growth is not just about moving up, it is about moving forward with intention.

On the flip side, patience without ambition can leave you stagnant, waiting endlessly for what some people call "the right time," which never comes. Without ambition to light a fire under you, it is easy to get comfortable and settle for less than what you're truly capable of achieving. Look around you, and you will realize that you are surrounded by countless patient people without ambition.

Which side of this spectrum are you on right now? Are you more ambitious than patient? Or do you have a healthy balance of both forces?

When patience and ambition come together, they form a powerful dynamic—a subtle dance if you will, where ambition leads with bold steps and patience keeps the rhythm steady. Ambition creates momentum, propelling you toward your vision, while patience ensures that every move is deliberate, measured, and sustainable. In this dance, rushing only leads you in circles.

I have witnessed this dance of patience and ambition many times, not only in my own career but also in the teams I have worked with. In the kitchen, there's an unspoken truth: mastering your craft demands relentless years of grit, repetition, and refinement. The best chefs don't settle; they live their ambition day in and day out. They push themselves and their team to the edge, innovate without apology, and chase new heights. I have worked for them and I have worked with them, and ultimately, I have become one of them. We know one thing: you cannot shortcut your way to greatness. Perfection takes time, whether that's nailing a dish, running a flawless service, or leading a team that doesn't miss a beat. I am talking about balance; I am also referring to pushing limits while embracing the grind.

Growth is not rushed. It is earned.

In the fast-paced world of hospitality, where the pressure to perform is constant, this balance becomes even more critical. The drive to succeed can sometimes lead us to take shortcuts or rush through key steps in our own development. But the individuals and businesses that truly stand the test of time are those that respect both ambition and patience. They understand that the best results come from a relentless pursuit toward greatness and a deep trust in the process itself, no matter how long it takes. Together, patience and ambition create one of the best foundations for sustainable success. So, trust the process and let your growth happen at its natural pace. Learn to dance!

At La Cendrée, the Italian restaurant in Courchevel, it was evident that I wasn't where I truly belonged, even though I ended up making the best of it. My ambition, which had always driven me to aim higher, kept urging me to search for something more aligned with my goals. Every day, I felt the pull to move on. But rather than giving in to those feelings, I made the conscious decision to harness that ambition and trust the process unfolding before me. It was very difficult to stay, especially since I could just *choose* to move on, but my unwillingness to break my commitment was the stronger force. Everyone who knows me knows how stubborn I can be, tenacious even. So, instead of rushing off,

I prepared myself for the next chapter of my journey. I corrected my trajectory and focused heavily on finding the next opportunity—then I had to trust that the right one would come. I spent most of my free time applying, knowing deep down that I wanted to be in Michelin star kitchens.

The transition between Courchevel's winter season and St. Tropez's summer season was a well-known path for hospitality professionals, so I made that my forward focus. I applied to every Michelin star restaurant within twenty-five miles of St. Tropez. I didn't even care if they were hiring; I just mailed out my resume and cover letter. At the time, the key to attracting a restaurant's attention was a handwritten resume and cover letter, so that's what I did, probably a dozen times over. My persistence paid off when I was offered a position at Lei Mouscardins, a 2 Michelin star restaurant under Chef Laurent Tarridec. It was the next step I had been looking for, and it reaffirmed my belief that patience and ambition can work together to lead to something even greater, something I desperately craved to stay true to who I was.

As we move forward together, I want you to remember this: the journey often demands more—more endurance, adaptability, and strength—when the weight to keep going feels heaviest. And this will happen more times in your career than you can count, so brace yourself, be ready, and let time do its work to help you actively face the challenges ahead. Patience prepares us, but resilience is what carries us through the tough moments, the moments when pressure rises, when everything seems to be moving faster than we can handle. In those moments when we're being tested, resilience becomes our lifeline. And it's in those moments when patience transforms into resilience and we find a way to grow stronger from the heat, not merely withstand it. When you learn to dance with patience and ambition, you're learning to dance with fire—and resilience refines that dance into an unstoppable flame.

CHAPTER 4

RECIPE FOR RESILIENCE: THRIVING UNDER PRESSURE

Resilience has always been deeply ingrained in me, and I've heard this reflected time and time again from close mentors and co-workers alike. It is more than a skill I've developed; resilience has become a defining part of my identity. So many challenges I have faced in my career have tested my limits, from high-pressure kitchens, to learning a new language on the spot, to moments of professional doubt. Yet, it is in those moments that I have discovered what resilience truly means. It is so much more than bouncing back. You must absorb the pressure, as if it does not affect you; you must embrace the setbacks, like you knew they were coming your way all along; and you must transform all of that into fuel for your growth.

Resilience is not merely about surviving tough times; when

you are resilient, you are in a position to thrive in those tough times, finding strength when everything around you is going "down" and unraveling. Every so-called "failure" I've faced in my life has shaped me, not just as a professional but as a person. Resilience is the quality I value and admire the most about myself because it has allowed me to push beyond what I thought I was capable of. It has helped me carve out a career built on persistence and an obsessive belief in my ability to keep growing no matter what was thrown at me…figuratively *and* literally.

Resilience is the backbone of a growth mindset. It is the invisible thread that will hold together the highs and lows of your professional journey. In moments of pressure and adversity, resilience keeps you moving forward when quitting seems like the easiest choice. Pressure is inevitable, that is a reality, especially in hospitality. You will have to push through the high stakes of a project, you will have to navigate career uncertainty, and you will have to work hard to master a specific skill required for your new role. The weight of expectation will feel overwhelming, and that's a promise!

That's where resilience comes in with the ability to transform adversity into an opportunity for growth. It is within these moments of strain that you will find your true strength—one you didn't know you had that's been there all long…waiting patiently for you. But thriving under pressure requires a conscious decision to persist through discomfort; it is not a passive act or something that just happens. If you hold on to the belief that there's transformative value in hardship, however, then no matter the difficulty, you will emerge transformed on the other side.

4.1 INVITATION TO THE UNAVOIDABLE TRIAL

The glamorous coastal town of St. Tropez is located in the French Riviera in the Provence-Alpes-Côte D'Azur region of southern France. Once a humble fishing village, it transformed into a symbol of luxury, attracting celebrities, artists, and wealthy travelers from around the world. The town is famous for its stunning beaches and fancy beach clubs that cater to jet-set visitors. *Le Vieux Port*, or The Old Port, is often filled with multimillion-dollar yachts, adding to the town's reputation as a playground for the rich and famous. During summer nights, the port of St. Tropez comes alive with a magical, almost electric atmosphere.

I remember being there as if it was yesterday, and I loved every bit of it! The warm Mediterranean air was filled with the sound of electro-pop music, laughter, and the clinking of glasses from the bustling cafes, bars, and upscale restaurants lining the waterfront. Luxury yachts draped with twinkling lights docked along the harbor, creating a backdrop of elegance and extravagance. People strolled along the promenade, some dressed in chic designer outfits, others opting for the effortless elegance of the Cote D'Azur lifestyle. And then there was me, a hospitality worker attempting to blend in—armed with the perfect mix of enthusiasm and a shirt that *almost* said, "I belong here."

The vibe of St. Tropez is probably its best attribute: festive yet laid-back, with a mix of locals, artists, international visitors, and celebrities enjoying the vibrant nightlife. Street performers, musicians, and artists often set up along the quay, adding to the lively and creative energy. I could not get enough of that place back then.

When I was there, I worked at the restaurant Lei Mouscardins, a 2 Michelin star restaurant under Chef Laurent Tarridec. This restaurant offered a truly memorable experience in the heart of St. Tropez. It was perched on the edge of the old port, offering breathtaking panoramic views of the Mediterranean Sea, especially as the sun set behind the twinkling yachts docked nearby. The interior of the restaurant exuded understated luxury, its elegant, soft-toned décor accented with amazing and expensive paintings from local artists. The atmosphere was serene at all times, offering diners a sense of exclusivity. This place was well established and so much more than a destination for haute cuisine. Seafood was definitely the star of the menu, and you would not expect it any other way when you are seated just a few feet from the water. The menu was rooted in traditional French cuisine but elevated with Tarridec's creative and refined techniques. It was a blend of elegance, simplicity, and utmost precision, allowing the quality and simplicity of the ingredients to shine through. His bouillabaisse, the best traditional Provençal fish stew in St. Tropez, was such a delicacy! It was elevated to a fine-dining level, with perfectly cooked rock fish and shellfish in a rich flavored broth, served with a side of Rouille and toasted sourdough bread.

I was hired as a *commis* chef, or line cook, at Lei Mouscardins for the summer season. I was at the fish section under the direct leadership of a *chef de partie*, or dinner cook—someone who had more experience than me. The fast pace, the high expectations, and the precision of the Michelin-starred environment filled me with a sense of purpose again. I felt at home. There were eleven of us in the kitchen, plus Chef Laurent Tarridec when he deigned to join us for service.

I remember one day in particular: July 14 was *Fete Nationale*, France's equivalent of July 4 in the US. We knew it was going to be one of the busiest days of the year. The air was charged with anticipation when we arrived at 6 a.m., ready for the "war" we knew was coming. Chef Tarridec, however, was nowhere to be found. He arrived about thirty minutes before lunch service in a sour mood. He barely greeted anyone, and as we were gearing up for the madness ahead, he dropped a bombshell: he was shuffling all of us to different stations. No warning, no explanation. Just pointing fingers and giving orders. "You—meat station. You—garde manger. You're on fish now." When he got to me, he didn't even flinch. "Franck, you are off fish. You are doing meat tonight too," and then shouted a few times, "Routine is the ally of complacency!" Just like that.

As Chef Tarridec stood there, arms crossed and face set with a smirk as he delivered his last-minute decision to move us around, it was clear he was not looking for discussion; he was testing us. The kitchen froze for a second, trying to process the chaos before the doors opened. But no one dared question it. My mind raced and I felt my pulse quicken. *Routine is the ally of complacency?!* I thought to myself after listening to Chef Tarridec, almost in disbelief. His statement didn't add up in my head. Routine, to me, was about discipline. It was about consistency. It was how we perfected our craft—through repetition, refining our techniques, and becoming more precise with each service. Yet, there we were, on the busiest day of the year, getting thrown into the deep end.

I had worked hard to master my role at the fish section, but now I was standing in front of the meat station, staring at cuts I barely knew how to handle in the context of this menu. The dishes were simple enough but became complex without any kind of preparation. The timing was horrible, and I had no clue how I was going to pull this off. Panic started to creep in, but I knew I couldn't let it take hold. Honestly, though, I didn't even have time to be in panic mode.

In the kitchen, service waits for no one. As the minutes ticked down, I scrambled to find my place—mentally running through and trying to absorb the recipes I had seen others execute, trying to remember the plating, the sauces, the garnishes. I found myself asking the line cook that was there before me, but I could see him drowning in the garde-manger station, so I opted to figure things out on my own. The first tickets came in, and chaos erupted.

My hands were moving, but my mind was still catching up.

The meat station was a dance I had yet to learn, but I had to perform anyway; there was no way I would be the one to bring down the team, not today! My adrenaline was pumping, my mind fighting for control, and the only way forward was to adapt. Neither service nor the guests who were paying for their experiences cared about how I felt. This situation demanded resilience, and I had no choice but to find it within me.

As the orders piled up, mistakes were inevitable. But I kept pushing, refusing to let frustration break my focus. Chef Tarridec had thrown us into the fire, and I knew the only way out was to keep cooking food—methodically, patiently, and with all the focus I could muster. By the middle of service, I started to find a rhythm, imperfect as it was. My mistakes lessened, and my hands, guided by muscle memory and willpower, began to produce plates that met the standard of the Chef at the pass. The service dragged on for what felt like days, but gradually the storm began to clear.

As the last plates went out and we reached the end of the lunch service, I was physically and mentally drained. But I prided myself in still standing, still in front of the meat station. I had not broken; I had adapted. I had learned. That day was far from perfect, but it reminded me of one undeniable truth, and I walked away with a promise to myself I've not broken since. The truth? Resilience is not about failure or discomfort; it's about endurance, about finding the strength to keep going, especially when everything is falling apart. And the promise? Well, I would never let myself be in a similar situation again, so I decided to learn all the stations moving forward, regardless of which one was "mine."

In the end, Chef Tarridec's decision to shuffle us around, as maddening as it was, forced me to confront a new level of pressure. I needed to face the unknown and find the ability to thrive in it. Resilience was not a deliberate choice that day; it was a necessity.

Adversity often feels like being pushed to the limit—the pressure is undeniable, and the discomfort is real, both mentally and physically. Just as challenges build strength in us, they also refine our capabilities and mindset. Adversity, looked at this way, is not to be feared; it must be embraced. True growth is born from discomfort—that is the fastest, most guaranteed path for it. On your professional journey, you will experience setbacks, moments of rejection, and times when the weight of the situation is pressing down so hard on you that it feels unbearable. That is when you must make a decision, and it's totally up to you which direction to go: into the fire of resilience or out. And sometimes, like that day I found myself at the meat station, resilience doesn't feel like a choice at all; you simply make it through and find that you're a different person on the other side.

In the world of hospitality, you must get used to these refining moments, or at least come to expect them, because they're part of the landscape. Staffing challenges, for example, are never-ending due to high turnover and the need to fill shifts on short notice. Dealing with guests' expectations is another constant challenge.

You're essentially on stage every day. Despite the aim to deliver exceptional service, complaints about food, timing, and/or atmosphere are an inevitable part of navigating these high expectations. Then there are operational issues, equipment malfunctions, and supply chain disruptions—any one of these can throw off a carefully planned weekend of service, forcing the staff to improvise under pressure. Regulatory challenges, like health inspections, have a knack for showing up at the perfect moment—right when you're juggling a dozen things, none of which include three free hours minimum to spare. It's almost like the inspector knows your schedule better than you do. I'm still not sure if it's luck, timing, or some sixth sense they have…but the scars from these "surprise visits" still linger!

I can go on and on with examples, but I think you're starting to get the picture: hospitality is stressful and full of very real, sometimes painful challenges—often by design. The pain runs deeper than just discomfort or fatigue. It can take many forms, testing you mentally, emotionally, even breaking you down if you're not prepared. So, let's dig further into resilience to see what it offers us on our journey of growth!

4.2 NO PAIN, NO GAIN

What do you do when you're going through a heavy day? Or when self-doubt, fear of failure, or exhaustion creep in? And what do you do when your mind starts playing tricks on you, amplifying every setback and making you feel isolated, like no one understands your situation or is willing to help? The deeper you push, the more pain emerges, making you question if you are strong enough to continue. That is what I refer to as "mental pain."

Mental pain, for me, is that moment when everything feels like it's closing in: a storm of doubt, frustration, and negativity that blinds me to anything beyond it. It is more than just a bad day. It is the suffocating weight of feeling stuck, like I have hit a wall so hard that I begin questioning everything. *Why am I doing this? Why is it so hard? Why can't I push through?* My thoughts pile up like bricks, each one heavier than the last, until it feels impossible to see a way forward. In those moments, every step forward is harder than the last. Then exhaustion sets in—the kind that makes me wonder if I have anything left to give. *Maybe I have gone far enough. Maybe this is where I'm supposed to stop.* The power of *yet* feels distant, overpowered by the constant nagging voice in my head that says, *You are not ready. You are not enough.*

Then there is the loneliness. You are struggling, but your pride keeps you from asking for help because admitting that you need help feels like a major failure. Instead, you find yourself wishing for someone to notice. *Why can't they see the struggle this is for me? Why is no one helping?* Frustration turns outward, and the blame starts: *If only I had more support. Why does it feel like I'm carrying this alone while others are just chilling?* But deep down, you know this isn't really about them. It's about you reaching your breaking point. When frustration boils over, you lash out at everything and everyone around you. But the lesson in those moments is profound: the real battle is within. That suffocating heaviness? It's not just the work; it is the mental strain of carrying it all, believing you can't drop it, and not knowing how to ask for help without being mocked or laughed at.

This mental pain is a signal that you are closer to a breakthrough than you realize. The pressure is also a gift. Yes, you read that correctly: the struggle itself is a gift. It is refining you, preparing you for the next step in your growth. But this gift requires persistence to realize its true value. It requires the choice to show up every day, especially on the days when everything feels too hard. You must believe with conviction that the pain you are facing today is shaping the strength you will need tomorrow.

Following my season in St. Tropez, I was offered an opportunity to leave France and go explore the world for a contract of six months. I told myself that maybe going to a tropical destination instead of returning to Courchevel was the better choice, and when I put them side by side, the decision was clear. Palm trees, beaches, and absolutely no snow at all. So there I was, on my way to the airport after a few days at home to swap my clothes. I packed a new bag and moved to St. Barthelemy, or St. Barts, a small, exclusive island in the French West Indies known for its white sand beaches, turquoise waters, and luxurious ambiance. The island is rich in French culture, with boutique shops, fine dining, and beautiful colonial architecture. It was like the St.

Tropez of the Caribbean—another favorite destination among the elite.

I was just twenty years old, stepping onto a miniscule island in the Caribbean that felt a world away from home. This was my first time being so far from my family—more than just several hours, I was now several flights away. I had accepted the position of pastry chef at a luxury resort called Guanahani Resort & Spa; it was not a Michelin-star-rated establishment, but it was luxurious nonetheless. The resort, located between Marigot Bay and Grand Cul-de-Sac on the northeastern shores, offered vibrant ocean views. Its colorful cottages, scattered among tropical gardens, provided both privacy and tranquility. With fine dining, a sumptuous spa, and beachfront access, Guanahani Resort & Spa balanced island charm with sophisticated elegance, making it a top choice for relaxation and understated luxury.

Once I was there, I did not care much about being on an idyllic island; I was driven and ambitious. I dove into work headfirst, and I worked like I had something to prove, pushing myself harder than ever. I was given an opportunity, and I was not about to waste it. I was putting in crazy hours and the pressure to deliver was intense, though some of it was self-inflicted. For some reason, I wanted to prove that I could be a pastry chef of a luxurious resort at just twenty years old. I had many early mornings, often before the sun rose, and I worked well into the night most of the time. The property catered to high-end guests, and every detail mattered. My role in the pastry kitchen was ensuring that anything with some level of "sweetness" to it was not only flawless but also creative and memorable. I worked with precision so that each pastry or dessert came out perfectly. That was the job, and I took it very seriously.

As I was adjusting to the workload, finding my rhythm in the chaos, I received news that shook me. My grandfather, Jacques, someone I was very close to, had passed away. I did not know what to do. All of a sudden, the distance from home felt overwhelming—I was devastated when I realized that, even if I caught the next flight, I would not make it back in time for the funeral. It felt impossible to reconcile: I was so far from everything familiar, and I felt very alone. After a difficult conversation with my father, I made the decision to stay on the island. It was not easy, and I did not fully realize how much that loss would affect me. I was already drained from the pace of work, but now I was emotionally unavailable as well, having to process losing someone so close without getting the chance to say goodbye. It was an incredibly hard time. Every day felt like a battle between showing up for the job I had committed to and dealing with the weight of emotions I refused to confront. But I kept going. I had made a decision, and I had to live with it. I had a responsibility—to myself, to the team, and to the role I had worked so hard to earn.

The persistence it took to show up every single day to work a ridiculous number of hours was unlike anything I had experienced before. Some days, it felt impossible to gather the energy to push through and focus on my work. But I realized that showing up, despite the struggle, was my only way forward. I was not simply going through the motions; I was battling through something deeply personal while trying to uphold the professional standards I had set for myself.

Looking back, I realize the power of my persistence. When life became heavy, when I felt like it was too much, I still found something within me to keep moving forward. I am not suggesting you follow my same path—each person's journey is different—but that experience taught me something essential. Even though it was hard to show up and put in endless work hours, even when I felt like I had nothing left to give, there was a strength in persistence that carried me through. I understood that persistence would not make the burden easier, but it did make it possible to keep going. And that, in itself, is a powerful thing.

Persistence is what separates those who move forward from those who falter. There is no point trying to achieve perfection or expecting immediate results in our most painful and challenging times; in these moments, we must simply keep persisting with focus, effort, and resilience. When we embrace adversity and continue to persist despite the setbacks, we eventually find ourselves moving steadily toward our goals.

In hospitality, the grind can feel never-ending. Long hours, tough crowds, high expectations—this is where mental pain thrives. But the beauty of persistence in this context is that through each service, each moment when you do not give in, you are not just getting through the day, you are *growing*. The discomfort you feel, the strain on your mind—leaning into these difficulties *is* the journey of resilience, getting you through the moment itself and preparing you for whatever comes next. And when you push through the mental barriers, you begin to understand what it means to thrive under pressure.

4.3 WHERE TRUE CHARACTER IS FORGED

You do not have to work in a luxury hotel or Michelin-star-rated restaurant to be exposed to real pressure. For many professionals, the pressure of a demanding job is a daily battle. It's like there's always a clock ticking, always an expectation to meet, always the feeling of barely keeping your head above water. I've been there. Many of us have. True resilience goes beyond simply enduring these pressures—you must thrive in the face of them, rising stronger with each test. The kind of tests that make you question whether you are cut out for the journey you have chosen. I want to assure you that you are; but you must learn how to thrive within the journey, letting the pressure shape you, not break you.

Pressure can be our greatest teacher because it has the power to reveal what we're truly made of. Thriving under it does not mean you won't feel its intensity. It means learning to channel that intensity into performance, using that pressure as the very force that propels you to a higher level, unlocking new creativity, precision, and leadership.

In a kitchen environment, you'll find yourself pushing to deliver experiences beyond expectations. During those intense services, every second counts and the stakes feel impossibly high. There may be a chef behind you, or maybe (and this never gets old) the whole restaurant seems to have been seated at once. You can't let the team down either, and the pressure of not bringing everyone down with you feels like a heavy weight on top of it all. During these moments, I anchor myself by focusing on just one priority—the next plate, the next move. This shrinks the chaos ever so slightly and brings me back to execution. But that doesn't eliminate the discomfort.

The goal of thriving through these pressure-filled moments, however, isn't about eliminating the feelings of fear and doubt that accompany them. Thriving does not equal fearlessness. We must feel that fear, that doubt, and still choose to step up. Welcome the fear as part of the process, driving you to stay sharp and fuel your determination.

Shifting from surviving to thriving requires a proactive mindset. A mindset that anticipates challenges and meets them head on. This shift happened for me when I stopped seeing pressure as something happening *to* me and started seeing it as something happening *for* me instead. Every service, every demanding guest, every unexpected twist became a chance to grow, to stretch beyond what I thought I could handle. Another way I built that mindset was reviewing these pressure-filled moments once they were over; I would ask myself what worked, what did not, and what I would do differently next time. That is how I built readiness, not just resilience.

But when the pressure is on, when things feel like they're slipping through your fingers, the only thing that matters is your next move. I've been in the middle of the chaos, time and time again, questioning myself. But self-doubt never solved the problem—handling it did. Action made all the difference, plain and simple. When you are deep in it, wondering if you can handle it, let me tell you this: there will be no room to sit back and analyze. You must act. You cannot wait for the perfect conditions or hope that the pressure lets up before digging in and doing the work. What matters when you're in the fire is that you keep moving forward, making the best decisions you can in the moment and owning the consequences of your actions afterward, both the good and the bad. That is where true resilience comes to light— that is when true character is forged.

And when the clock is ticking and the pressures mounting, trust the foundation you've already built. Rely on the preparation, the skills, the discipline you have honed, because that is exactly what is going to carry you through.

Doubt will start creeping in; do not engage with it. I remember quietly wondering if I truly belonged: if I was good enough, sharp enough, worthy enough to stand among the chefs I looked up to. Even when things were going well, there was this constant hum of insecurity beneath the surface, like I was one mistake away from being exposed as a fraud. I carried those doubts with me, pretending they weren't there while they ate at me from the inside. But I have learned that doubts don't need to be silenced; they just need to be put in their place. Keep showing up, and let your actions speak louder than the noise in your head.

Focus on pushing through. Take the immediate next step on the task at hand, and keep going, one step at a time, one decision at a time. The ones who come out stronger from the forge of pressure are not the ones with all the answers, they are the ones who don't get caught up in second-guessing themselves. In choosing to act, you will discover just how capable you are, and, most importantly, how this ability was there inside of you from the beginning.

In moments of pressure, your next move defines your path, so choose action, not hesitation…and thrive!

4.4 YOU CAN'T STOP THE UNSTOPPABLE

I will never forget the intensity of working in Michelin-star-rated restaurants. It is too often glamorized—the white tablecloths, the perfectly plated dishes, the prominence that can come from being part of the elite. What is neither glamorized nor displayed is the grueling reality behind it all. It is an environment that demands nothing less than perfection, every single day. The standards are not just high, they are nearly impossible to reach. But that is the point. No one is there to meet expectations; they are there to exceed them, and I've had the most exhilarating and exhausting experiences of my career in this environment.

The pressure in Michelin-star-rated kitchens is not something we talk about, it is the air we breathe. Every single person has their role to play, and if you fail to deliver, there is no hiding. Everyone in the kitchen feels it. And everyone is looking at you all at once. The tension is palpable. In those kitchens, there is no such thing as good enough, or as Chef Olivier Bellin would say, "Good enough is not good enough for people like us." Every dish is scrutinized, every detail must be perfectly executed, and every second counts. Talk about pressure...but it is designed to be this way. I learned the value of resilience in these kitchens. And the value of discipline—the relentless routine of doing the same thing over and over again until it becomes second nature. That is, unless you work for Chef Laurent Tarridec in St. Tropez, where routine is a synonym for complacency.

Beyond the expectation of perfection and the discipline required, there's constant scrutiny as well. Working in a Michelin kitchen means you are always being judged—by the chef, by your colleagues, even by yourself. Any day could be the day a Michelin inspector walks through the door. You do not know who they are or when they will come, but you prepare as if they are always watching. It is a level of pressure that few outside the industry can understand. Then, after putting yourself under that level of duress, you come to a mind-blowing realization: the person judging you has less knowledge than you as a chef! The whole system is nonsensical! Nevertheless, you persist. You exceed expectations. You deliver.

When I first started, I was eager to prove myself. I thought excellence in the kitchen was all about talent and skills, but I quickly realized it was about so much more than that. Michelin kitchens have a way of not just testing your skills but testing your spirit too. There were nights where I would be running on four hours of sleep, my body aching from the night before, my mind exhausted from knowing that we had yet to start the weekend and I could barely function. But I had to find the energy to push through. And not just push through; I had to be on my best game. After a few years in the industry, quitting didn't cross my mind because I wholeheartedly knew that quitting wouldn't help me grow. I learned to push past my limits and discover a new level of determination within myself.

One of the hardest lessons, though, was not pushing past my limits but accepting that I would make mistakes along the way. After countless hours of work, endless striving for perfection, constantly being "on" from the moment I arrived until the moment I left, I often felt like I had given everything I had. And yet, I would still fall short on an important service, or I would mess up a VIP table. I have sent out undercooked meat, missed critical allergies, and once completely forgot to fire a course for a high-profile guest, only realizing my mistake when I noticed the table staring at each other for several minutes without food in front of them. Those moments stung deeply, not just because of the mistakes themselves but because of what they triggered in me: shame, self-doubt, the fear that maybe I was not as capable as I thought.

But that is where I found my lesson: instead of letting these mistakes defeat me, I would double down and exert twice the effort. I would question everything. *Where can I improve? What details am I missing?* That is when I truly saw the power of resilience and unstoppable growth in action. Challenges would always come my way, especially in hospitality. But when I faced them head on, when I refused to be stopped by the pressure or the setbacks or the rejections, I came out on the other side with a deeper sense of purpose and strength. I have always believed that you can't stop the unstoppable, and I have lived by that motto my entire career. The inner voice that says "watch me" or "challenge accepted" is what drives me to continue pushing, to continue growing day in and day out, because I know so well that every obstacle is just another opportunity to emerge stronger.

That is the essence of my story of working over ten years in Michelin-star-rated restaurants. Some of the best in the world. It was not just a job; it was a lifestyle. I learned to live and breathe the pursuit of excellence, and it was not all glamorous. It was raw, it was real, and it was often brutal. But when I made it through, when I came out on the other side of another day, I knew I'd been a part of something extraordinary. Yes, I had to love the food, the stars, and the prestige. But it took persistence and resilience to be one of the last ones standing, sometimes *literally*. It is that journey, and the countless moments of doubt and triumph I encountered along the way, that shaped me into someone who can handle whatever comes next.

Every time you face adversity and you choose to persevere, you are adding to your reserve of strength. Resilience is cumulative; no experience of thriving under pressure is ever wasted because each one, by its very nature, inspires growth. Go through enough of these experiences and you develop a natural sense of confidence and readiness, knowing you can face whatever happens next—expected or not. Anything you practice, you will get good at, so keep persisting, keep moving forward. Be adaptable in your methods, stay fluid in your approach, but never stop progressing—and growth will come from every turn and every painful, thrilling opportunity.

CHAPTER 5

CRAFTING CHARACTER: A STORY OF ADAPTABILITY

Adaptability is an essential craft in the process of growth, particularly in the fast-paced and unpredictable world of hospitality. Without it, progress stalls and challenges become insurmountable. With it, your instincts sharpen, allowing you to face the unexpected with increasing confidence and creativity. When you become adaptable, you start to feel steady, even outside your comfort zone. In fact, when you embrace change as a tool for growth, it becomes harder to define where your comfort zone is, because you're so used to adjusting outside of it to meet whatever challenges arise. Those who actively develop adaptability build a different kind of resilience. They're not just surviving, they're not just thriving—they're evolving into stronger, more flexible people, better equipped to face whatever's next in their journey.

Like any craft, becoming more adaptable takes dedication and a willingness to refine over time, until it becomes a key part of who you are. Thinking of yourself as an adaptable person influences how you tackle challenges; clarity and purpose hone themselves in your newfound identity as someone who can learn, grow, and adapt through anything.

In today's world, being adaptable is more necessary than ever. The speed of life, driven by social media and instant gratification, demands quick fixes and immediate results. Society is losing patience (and it's not changing anytime soon), and in this environment, adaptability becomes a true differentiator. The pressure to keep up can be overwhelming. But those who master the craft navigate the chaos with intention. They start to anticipate, adjust, and evolve, sometimes without even realizing it. And the best part? For those who truly embrace this craft, adapting to whatever a situation demands starts to feel effortless.

5.1 THE UPSIDE OF DISRUPTION

In 2008, a few years after my time in St. Barts, I arrived in Arles, in the heart of Provence, France. Arles radiates a unique blend of rustic charm and timeless elegance. With its sun-soaked streets, it stands as a living museum of history and culture, where ancient Roman ruins meet the vibrancy of modern life. The remnants of its past are everywhere, from the grandeur of the Roman amphitheater—still hosting bullfights and performances today—to the ancient columns that whisper stories of a bygone era. Even the light there feels different; famously captured by Vincent van Gogh during his time in Arles, it fills the narrow streets and squares with a golden glow, as if his presence still lingers in the cobblestone alleys.

I vividly remember the market in Arles—one of the largest and most energetic in all of France. Going to the market was always an event. Stalls overflowed with vibrant produce: sun-ripened tomatoes, herbs, local cheeses, delicacies with charcuterie from the region, seafood fresh from the Mediterranean, bottles of olive oil—the very essence of Provencal life. I can still smell the scent of lavender and savory herbs mixing with the aroma of fresh bread and the sounds of vendors calling out their offerings in the thick accent of southern France. This small, sun-drenched city had a timeless quality to it, merging the old with the new. And it was against this backdrop that I stepped into the creative and intense world of L'Atelier de Jean-Luc Rabanel.

L'Atelier de Jean-Luc Rabanel was a culinary laboratory of creativity and refinement. The restaurant's concept revolved around a dynamic and unpredictable dining experience. The space itself was intimate and modern, with a minimalist aesthetic that emphasized the artistry of the cuisine. The open, almost gallery-like feel of the restaurant's interior starkly contrasted the bold, red tables—an intense pop of color against the otherwise minimalist décor, neutral walls, and simple, clean lines. The soft lighting created a warm and inviting atmosphere, and the open kitchen showcased the energy and precision of the culinary team.

The restaurant had no traditional menu, offering eighteen *touches de gouts* instead—small taste sensations that highlighted seasonal ingredients and showcased Rabanel's innovative culinary style. These dishes could shift from one service to the next, sometimes in a matter of hours. Every day was an adventure, to say the least.

Chef Jean-Luc would visit the local market in Arles in the early morning, hunting for the freshest seasonal ingredients. What he brought back could instantly alter the menu. By lunchtime, the kitchen was already buzzing with anticipation as new ingredients were laid out, each one signaling a shift in our approach. The menu was always in flux, evolving with whatever caught the chef's eye, from heirloom vegetables to wild herbs, each ingredient telling a story of the region.

This was no ordinary restaurant—it was a place that demanded total adaptability, pushing everyone beyond what we thought we could achieve. When I joined L'Atelier, the restaurant had already earned its first Michelin star and was gaining a reputation for culinary innovation. The moment I stepped into its small kitchen, the energy was palpable and infectious. We even had a camera mounted near the ceiling that captured the entire kitchen in a single shot, with a monitor by the front door of the restaurant so that passersby on Cobblestone Street could watch us in action as we prepared the menu of the day. This was not just another kitchen; it was a creative "workshop" where tradition met bold experimentation. The team buzzed with activity, their movements precise and their focus unbroken.

Chef Jean-Luc Rabanel himself radiated a unique charisma—culinary genius combined with a whirlwind of culinary chaos, an unpredictable force of nature in the kitchen. His energy was always electric, sometimes wild, and often erratic; yet, it was precisely this controlled chaos that fueled his brilliance. Sometimes his passion seemed like pure madness. I remember one evening in particular, just minutes before service. Chef was standing over a dish we had plated dozens of times before. Without warning, he ripped it apart with his bare hands, smeared the sauce off the plate, and muttered with his singing Gascon accent, *"Non, ça ne ressemble a rien, c'est plat."* ("No, it looks like nothing; it is flat.") Then, in a flurry of motion only he seemed to understand, he rebuilt it: restructured, raw, and bold. It was the kind of madness that bordered on obsession, but his creations—wild, daring, and unforgettable—proved that his culinary insanity was, in fact, pure brilliance in disguise.

Adding to this intensity, we were constantly short-staffed. The brigade was a revolving door. New recruits came in wide eyed and left hollowed out after only a few days, unable to keep up with the unstoppable pace and impossible standards. I still remember one of them throwing down his apron mid-service, shouting, *"Vous êtes tous fous ici!"* ("You're all insane here!") He was not wrong. And yet, those of us who stayed—people like

Florent Courriol, who was crazy enough to come back after leaving once; Antoine Foezon, another "brother" from Brittany; and Bruno Laporte, a rare addition who managed to stick with us—we didn't just survive this environment, we fed off it. Every day was a high-wire act with no safety net, and somehow we found our rhythm in the madness. We became a small, irreducible unit. A team forged in heat, pressure, and a shared, almost delusional belief that perfection was just one more plate away. No matter how chaotic, no matter how hard the day hit us, we adapted. We were a little deranged, maybe, but we were all in. And together, we were unshakable. We refused to break.

When Chef Jean-Luc Rabanel was named "Chef of the Year" in the 2008 Gault-Millau guide, the pressure mounted. Every dish was scrutinized, and every service tested the limits of our skills. Chef Rabanel pushed us harder than ever before, refining techniques and demanding more precision. He was impossible to satisfy, almost suffocating at times. No matter how hard I pushed myself or how close I thought I was to meeting *his* standards, the goal felt just out of reach—like I was chasing an ever-moving target that I was simply not destined to catch. He left us with a constant sense of urgency and a nagging doubt that we were always falling short. Adaptability in this environment was not just a necessity but an art form.

As the days turned into weeks and then months, rumors swirled about the impending Michelin guide. Work demanded even more focus and resilience—everyone knew what was at stake. The menu continued to change at a breakneck pace, sometimes just hours before service. It was nuts! Customers booked months in advance, expecting the unexpected, and we had to deliver, fully immersed in the fast-paced rhythm of the kitchen—*his* kitchen!

Then one day, the news arrived: the second Michelin star had been awarded. A wild rush of emotions followed: relief, joy, pride, and a profound sense of accomplishment. I was so overwhelmed that I grabbed a chair from behind the pastry section and simply sat down. I am not sure how long I was there, but it felt like a couple days had passed with me quietly sitting on that chair. It was a victory earned through every market trip, every sleepless night, every dish crafted on the fly. That second star validated all the sacrifices, the long hours, and the moments when I had wondered if this path was for me, if I was pushing myself too far.

But this amazing accolade was not enough for Jean-Luc Rabanel that year. Opening the bistro A Côté that same year added more intensity to our schedule. We were no longer just maintaining one restaurant, we were running two. Preposterous! The constant adaptations did not stop, but neither did the sense of purpose that drove us. We barely acknowledged and appreciated reaching the second star. The restaurant was so booked that we had no time to really enjoy it. For Rabanel, it seemed that success was not about reaching the stars—it was about proving that adaptability and determination in the world of haute cuisine could lead to something truly extraordinary.

My time at L'Atelier profoundly shaped my character and my outlook; in the world of fine-dining, I learned, adaptability and the relentless pursuit of excellence are everything. Earning that second Michelin star—knowing it was the result of perseverance and absolute adaptability—remains one of the most rewarding moments of my career.

True adaptability begins when you learn to embrace disruption rather than resist it. Change, by its very nature, is unsettling. However, when you shift your mindset to view disruption as a catalyst for innovation and opportunity, you unlock your potential to lead with vision. In hospitality, disruption is commonplace—whether it's being constantly short-staffed, rolling with menu changes, or trying to earn a Michelin star. Think of disruptions not as roadblocks but as sparks that ignite creative solutions. When you face the unexpected—and I guarantee you, you will—don't just react. Recalibrate, then innovate. What will set you apart as an adaptable leader is your ability to greet these moments with extreme composure, creativity, and a deep well of unshakable calm.

5.2 THE ART OF FLUID EXPERTISE

"Think of yourself as water: fluid, ever-moving, and ready to take the shape of whatever container you find yourself in."

What is the art of fluid expertise? It's the mindset that our skills are never truly fixed; they're capable of expanding beyond traditional limitations. In fact, in a world that changes rapidly, staying fixed in one set of skills can limit our growth and impact. Fluidity means developing a versatile toolkit that allows us to move between roles, challenges, and environments with ease. We don't have to be good at everything, but the intention is to be ready for anything.

In my career, fluidity meant learning more than just my station. I studied how the pass worked, how the front-of-house communicated, and how to jump into each station. To develop this yourself, you could intentionally ask for cross-training or simply step into unfamiliar roles, even briefly, just to understand how the system flows. The more you expose yourself to different rhythms and responsibilities, the faster you build instinct and agility and the more fluid you become. This is particularly relevant in hospitality, where one day you might be managing a team, and the next day you're stepping into the kitchen to assist during the rush. Or, shortly after going to a productivity meeting about your labor cost, you now have to resolve a guest complaint with diplomacy and grace.

It's important to remember that fluidity is not about mastering every skill but about adapting, learning from every experience, and remaining curious even when things go off script. This mindset of constant motion keeps you both agile and humble, as there's always more room to grow.

Fluidity is probably the hardest skill to learn for leaders because it requires stepping out of comforting certainty and into the flow of constant change. Many leaders rise to their roles by mastering a specific set of skills or excelling in particular areas, and shifting from a position of expertise to one of continual learning can be deeply challenging. And, truth be told, ego and pride will certainly take a hit when leaders value fluidity—because the art of staying fluid means admitting when they don't know something, asking questions, and learning from others, even those they're leading.

I learned this firsthand at L'Atelier de Jean-Luc Rabanel. One afternoon, we were prepping for yet another last-minute menu change when I found myself completely out of my depth with a new vegetable-forward technique I had never seen before. Instead of pretending I knew what to do, I turned to Florent and asked, "How the hell are you making this work?" Without hesitation, he walked me through it—no ego involved, just focus. Moments like that were common with our team. Whether it was Antoine stepping into pastry to help me finish the service or Bruno switching stations mid-service to stabilize the entire line, we all relied on each other's strengths. That is what fluidity looks like in real time: not knowing everything, but knowing how to move, listen, and adapt. The leaders I've respected the most were not the ones who barked orders from the top, they were the ones in the trenches, asking the right questions, willing to be students all over again.

This humility can be difficult, especially for those who feel pressure to appear competent and confident. But fluidity requires staying open to feedback and seeing mistakes as part of the learning process rather than as a threat to authority. It also requires moving away from rigid structures, fixed strategies, and patterns. For many, this feels like stepping into chaos. I know from experience that this can feel uncomfortable because it disrupts the illusion of control that we, as leaders, are expected to maintain. For most chefs, there's still a huge opportunity within the industry to embrace fluidity. Embracing fluidity doesn't mean abandoning all plans; you can have a plan B *and* the understanding that plan C, D, or E might be even better and be willing to pivot accordingly. Embracing fluidity means leading with this vulnerability, showing that you too are evolving and learning. This can be perceived as a weakness, but the ability to flow with challenges rather than force solutions through sheer willpower alone is actually a strength. This was one of the most difficult lessons of my growth journey, and it only came much later in my career.

After L'Atelier de Jean-Luc Rabanel earned its second Michelin star, I was promoted to *second de cuisine*—Rabanel's right hand...for both restaurants. The weight of this promotion was both exhilarating and daunting. Suddenly, I was no longer just following directions; I was expected to lead, to make decisions, and to handle challenges with confidence *while* working the line since we were still short-staffed. Yet, despite my achievements, I found myself struggling.

My toolkit, while solid, lacked fluidity. I was rigid, hesitant to adapt on the fly, and uncomfortable showing any hint of vulnerability in my new role. I thought being second in command meant I needed to have all the answers. I thought I had to be an unshakable pillar of knowledge and strength, especially with new cooks joining the team. I remember a moment in pastry one night when I was clearly going down; tickets piling up as usual, components clearly not ready, my timing completely off. But I was too proud to call for help. I kept my head down, convinced I could muscle through it. I did not want to show weakness, especially in front of the rest of the team. After all, I was second in command.

At one point, Antoine walked by, leaned over the pastry station, and with his usual sarcastic grin said, "Are we not asking for help, Mr. Desplechin?" It was lighthearted, but it landed. I laughed it off in the moment, but deep down I knew he was right. By the time service ended, I had dragged the whole team behind. I realized I had not failed because I lacked skill but because I let pride outweigh my trust in the team. That experience taught me that true leadership is not about holding the line at all costs; it's about knowing when to loosen your grip, trust your team, and move forward together.

But letting go of my ego still felt impossible. There was constant internal pressure to be perfect, to never make mistakes. Appearing unsure was out of the question. When I connected the dots backwards, however, I could see this mindset created a barrier, not just between me and the team—even though we were very tight and became close friends—but also between me and the kitchen's natural rhythm. I became easily frustrated when things did not go according to plan, unable to bend with the unexpected challenges that came along with running both restaurants. I tried to control every aspect of every day, believing that leadership required absolute certainty. That led me to work stints of over twenty days in a row—no days off—several times since the bistro A Côté was open seven days a week.

The harder I held on, the more disconnected I felt—from the team, from the creative flow, even from myself. I easily blamed my exhaustion back then. I was in a challenging phase, a silent struggle where my pride and desire to excel clashed with the kitchen's demand for adaptability and humility. The kitchen was evolving, but I felt stuck, resisting the very change that had brought us to the exclusive list of being one of the top twenty best restaurants in the country.

Fluidity demands that we invest in a broader set of skills, moving beyond our core expertise to develop a more diverse and adaptable toolkit. This will take time, effort, and a willingness to step into the unfamiliar, all while maintaining the pressure of your regular responsibilities, but start as soon as you can, because you will inevitably need this larger toolkit. You'll have to set aside the notion of quick wins and short-term success as you embrace the art of fluid expertise and focus instead on long-term growth and development. The journey will not be straightforward—but neither is a river. It bends and adapts to obstacles, speeding up and slowing down as the terrain requires, but it never stops flowing.

Like a river, leaders who adapt, learn, and remain open to new approaches will thrive, but getting there means confronting deeply ingrained habits and existing beliefs about what it means to be in charge. There is no way around this; you must evolve from being the expert—always sure of the next move, always sure of the answers—into a guide who can navigate a path that is rarely straightforward. That is what it means to lead by example. In staying fluid yourself, you're encouraging others to follow, showing them that the way forward requires adaptability rather than unbending authority. The greatest leaders do not just direct, they demonstrate the courage to change; they embody the values they wish to see in others.

With fluidity in your skill set, you'll be able to move seamlessly across challenges, pivoting, innovating, and excelling in ever-changing environments across a range of competencies. You'll become more effective in the present and more prepared for future shifts too, knowing that each challenge is a chance to redefine yourself. Nothing remains static in this life. Why should you?

5.3 ONE ADAPTATION AT A TIME

At this point in the book, it's time to ask yourself some tough questions. Are you choosing to evolve? Or are you waiting for change to force your hand? Tomorrow morning (and every morn-ing) you will have a choice: Will you stay comfortable in what you already know? Or will you challenge yourself to step into the unknown? What outdated beliefs or ideas are holding you back right now? Are you still waiting for the perfect moment to make a decision? If not now, when?

Adaptability is an ongoing act of self-renewal, a way to rise each day with the honest intention of becoming more than you were the day before. It is the decision to remain open to new ideas and perspectives, to let go of what is no longer effective, and to seek out beliefs and actions that will serve you better. Holding on too tightly to one version of yourself or a single way of doing things can become a limitation. But it takes courage to evolve because doing so often feels uncertain or uncomfortable, or both. You will need to be fearless in the face of change, knowing that—in the ever-increasing speed of our daily lives—the pursuit of adaptability is the pursuit of excellence. It's never-ending, and there are no guarantees; today's victories do not guarantee to-morrow's success. What keeps you relevant is adapting to trends, expectations, and circumstances, seeing the cracks before they appear so that you can shift your strategy as needed. This evolu-tion, with all its unknowns, is a vital stage of growth.

Toward the end of my time at L'Atelier de Jean-Luc Rabanel, I appeared to be one of the calmest people under pressure—not because I wasn't affected by it but because I had trained myself to see challenges differently. I had developed an inner flexibility that allowed me to bend without breaking, to stand firm when necessary, and to pivot when circumstances demanded it. My confidence didn't come from knowing all the answers; it came from trusting my ability and the team's ability to navigate the unknown and emerge stronger each time.

I was so absorbed in the intensity of my daily responsibilities and tasks that Chef Rabanel started playing a game with me. He would call every hour, saying he was just a few minutes away. This became a regular occurrence, and the anticipation that he would arrive soon kept building; the kitchen buzzed with pressure. But he never showed up. At first, I was confused. Why did he keep promising his arrival and never show? Only later did I realize this was his way of testing me, seeing if I could handle the heat without the safety net of his presence. And it worked. Those calls pushed me to take ownership of every decision and trust my instincts. And it got me and the team to perform at the highest level, as if he were watching over our shoulders the entire time. It was a silent challenge, one that forced me to grow and adapt, with or without him.

It was also a tough evolution for me because it required humility, and at the time, I thought humility was only for those who didn't know they were right. I had to be willing to shed my old habits and embrace constructive criticism. I had many opportunities to practice this, including the time Chef Rabanel told me my technique was solid but my plating had no emotion. That was rough to hear, but he wasn't wrong. Instead of shutting down, I sat with his feedback, and the next day, I walked in with a different mindset—more open, more intentional, and ready to learn. In the end, adaptability is not about perfection; it's about becoming better than you were yesterday and about finding fulfillment in that progress. It's the journey, not the destination. Every iteration of yourself—and there will be many—is a step toward something greater.

As we move forward on our journey of *Relentless Growth*, remember that adaptability is not just a response to new situations. It is an action, a mindset, and a willingness to adjust, learn, and transform when the path shifts, even when that shift feels like failure. Those who cultivate adaptability understand that setbacks are often the first ingredients of transformation—and failure itself becomes a taste of growth in its rawest form.

CHAPTER 6

REDEFINING FAILURE: A TRANSFORMATIVE TASTE

I strongly believe there are just two kinds of people in this world: those who play it safe, avoiding failure at any cost, and those who face it head-on, using every stumble as a stepping stone. The first group never dares, never risks, and never grows. The second understands that failure is not a threat; it is the most powerful teacher, a necessary part of the path to greatness, and the only way to truly grow. Every once in a while, someone from the first group decides to venture over to the second group. When that person experiences what they perceive as "failure," it brings them to a decision: fall back, thinking they never should've left the first group to begin with because "failing" is too uncomfortable, or continue, realizing there's something to learn from this so-called "failure," and try again—not from scratch this time but from lived experience.

People often view failure as negative because of a mix of societal, psychological, and cultural influences that shape how we perceive setbacks. Society emphasizes achievement and visible success as the gold standard we should all aim for, starting all the way from early childhood. This focus creates a mindset where winning competitions (official or not), gaining recognition, and achieving measurable results become the ultimate goals, leading to the belief that failure is a mark of personal incompetence or lack of ability. The way education is structured—with a heavy focus on grades and standardized tests that reward success and penalize mistakes—reinforces this belief. All of these influences combined can easily make failure feel like a threat to our self-worth and accomplishments rather than a chance to actually learn. Learning, of course, should be the ultimate goal, not what everyone else deems "successful."

Nevertheless, the widespread belief that failure is a bad thing can lead to a sense of finality when we encounter setbacks, making it difficult to embrace them as valuable experiences. Failure becomes something to hide, to be ashamed of, reinforcing the idea that it defines a person's worth or capabilities. Culturally, stories of success are too often celebrated while the struggles, failures, and learning moments that happened along the way are severely downplayed. These narratives suggest that success comes easily to those who are naturally talented or capable. Failure then becomes associated with vulnerability; we end up thinking that if we fail we'll expose our limitations and imperfections to the world. This discomfort leads many to shy away from taking risks that might result in coming up short of the intended goal, preferring to play safe rather than face the emotional and social consequences of falling short.

When it comes to career, failure has long been a word that strikes fear into the hearts and minds of professionals. It's often viewed as the definitive mark of inadequacy or an irreversible endpoint. Yet, in the world of hospitality—where the pressure is constant and the unexpected can strike at any moment—failure is an inevitable part of the journey. And it's not something we need to fear. In fact, it's possible to reimagine failure as an ally, not an enemy—to see it not as a dead end but as the beginning of something even better.

6.1 BEYOND THE INSTINCTIVE FEAR

First things first, let's dismantle the deeply ingrained instinct to see failure as a barrier—a "no-go" signal that tells you to turn back, or worse, that you are unworthy of moving forward. Let me say that again, more emphatically this time, because this is where it all starts: **Failure is not a barrier. It is not a "no-go" signal telling you to turn back. Experiencing failure does not mean you are unworthy of moving forward.**

I want to emphasize that fearing failure is often instinctual.

In addition to it being ingrained in us since childhood, it is also a defense mechanism that protects us from the discomfort of facing our imperfections head-on. In that initial moment of failure, when emotions are raw, the setback feels very personal, magnified out of proportion, and final. We tend to wrap our worth in achievements, so any deviation from success feels like a hit to our very sense of self.

No matter how we approach failure, it still carries emotional weight. Every setback demands resilience; it asks us to lean into the discomfort and look for clues: What went wrong? How can we do better next time? When we feel overwhelmed by a mistake, it's often because we're focusing on the loss, not the lesson; we're fixated on what could have been or what did not go as planned. By focusing instead on what we can still gain from this perceived loss, we free ourselves to extract value from the experience. We are allowing ourselves to pause, take a step back, and separate the event from our identity. Each stumble then becomes less of a stop sign and more of a speed bump or detour on our path toward greatness.

In 2012, when my plane touched down on Kauai, the Garden Island, I couldn't help but recall that nerve-racking interview—the one that felt like a long shot from the start and where I somehow convinced them that my nonexistent English skills wouldn't be an issue. They must have seen something in me I didn't yet know was there, because there I was, a French pastry chef on a tropical island, about to learn just how far enthusiasm could take me when vocabulary would certainly fail.

Kauai is as captivating as it is timeless. Every view reveals something awe-inspiring; it feels like a hidden paradise brought to life by its people. The north shore is vibrant with rainforests, hidden waterfalls, and beaches lined with golden sands, each sight more breathtaking than the last. Princeville, calm and serene, is nestled into the landscape, as if it has always belonged there. Surrounded by the towering cliffs, sweeping beaches, and emerald forests, it feels like stepping into a world removed from the everyday.

What makes this place truly unforgettable, though, are the connections. *Yah, da locals on Kauai show me plenty Aloha, call me "braddah." Made da kine close friends ova dea, Kauai da home away from home, fo' real.* They welcomed me as a family immediately. The warmth here goes beyond small talk; it's in the way people wave as you pass by, the fabulous stories exchanged over plate lunches, and the sense of Aloha woven into every interaction. It's an island vibe that says, "You belong here," and each day you spend with the people of the island builds a bond that feels lasting and true. Life on Kauai is unhurried. It has two speeds: slow and...well, slower. Whether you're out for an early surf, hiking jungle paths, or sharing a Hawaiian breakfast in Hanalei Bay, the rhythm feels more like living than simply passing time.

The former St. Regis Princeville, now known as 1 Hotel Hanalei Bay, was a premier luxury destination on Kauai's North

Shore, dramatically set above the mesmerizing Hanalei Bay. Renowned for its expansive views of the Pacific and the majestic Na Pali Coast, the resort was the pinnacle of elegance infused with island charm. Its design captured the essence of Kauai, with grand windows and open spaces that invited the surrounding natural splendor to take center stage. The signature infinity pool, an iconic spot for guests to unwind, looked as if it merged with the waters of Hanalei Bay far below. Inside the St. Regis, Hawaiian-inspired interiors merged traditional island materials like Koa wood with sleek modern touches. Dining options like the Makana Terrace and Kauai Grill provided refined culinary experiences that celebrated Hawaii's flavors and Chef Jean-Georges Vongerichten's expertise. With its stunning coastal setting and intimate connection to the raw beauty of Kauai's landscape—probably one of the most stunning sunset experiences in the world—the Princeville property provided a rare blend of luxury and tranquil seclusion, where the natural world and refined comfort existed in harmony.

Stepping into the role of Executive Pastry Chef at the St. Regis Princeville without knowing a word of English felt like a sweet dream come true...or possibly a recipe for disaster. Turns out it was both! The language barrier did not just hang over my head; it filled every corner of my day. I could not ask questions, confirm details, or read an email, let alone respond to it. Even the simplest interactions felt like climbing a steep cliff with no handholds. Every word exchanged with my team felt like a test—one I often failed. For the team too, my inability to communicate clearly was a source of frustration. They could not rely on me to understand, and I could sense their patience thinning as we missed cues and repeated mistakes. I was the chef, yet I was failing them, adding weight to their already busy days. I could see in their glances, hear it in the sighs that followed every miscommunication, and feel it in the hesitancy with which they approached me. These were not just language issues, they were moments of doubt, for both them and me.

Each day, I had to step back from my instinct to let failure (or my fear of it) define my experience. At first, that instinct loomed large—each misunderstanding, each unspoken sentence, every unasked question felt like proof I did not belong. I had so many things to say, to address, to show, but I didn't yet have the vocabulary for any of it. I had to let go of the need to get everything right—and I had to learn that quickly. But I began to see another way forward. I realized that if I couldn't rely on words just yet, I had to lead through something more essential: presence, patience, and the unspoken language of shared effort.

The team needed someone who could remain calm, attentive, and adaptive—qualities that did not require perfect English, only the ability to stay present and steady, especially in the tough moments. I often made it a point to arrive at work as early as 5 a.m. and stay as long as anyone on the team, ensuring they felt my presence and had my full support available whenever they needed it. And, truth be told, I was also buried under a mountain of emails in a language I couldn't read, so I desperately needed this extra time. In lieu of knowing the right words, I focused on learning to read the kitchen through its movements, sounds, and glances. Every shift, I trained myself to listen beyond words, noticing the cadence of the team and the precise pace of production. I would watch how they moved, timing my own actions to support theirs, letting our shared dedication speak louder than any language. Gradually, I built a rhythm with the team while I kept at my English, which was improving daily, though nowhere near groundbreaking yet.

This new rhythm redefined my sense for leadership. I began to embrace some level of humility, realizing I was not there to prove myself but to prove that we could work together, even when the odds stacked high against us. It was through barely spoken words and quiet exchanges that we built an extraordinary amount of trust. By showing up with patience, respect, and persistence, we bridged the language barrier and learned to connect first through the universal language of shared commitment to our craft.

As the months passed, I came to understand that breaking beyond my instinctive fear of failure was not just about adapting to a language barrier or managing my role as Executive Pastry Chef. I also needed to redefine my inner response to uncertainty so I could push past the limits of what felt comfortable and safe. Fear, in its simplest form, told me to step back, to protect myself, to avoid situations that felt too challenging or new. But if I allowed that instinctive fear to dictate my actions, I would have missed out on everything I came to Kauai to achieve. That was never an option to me; I was there to grow.

Fear is completely natural, but it becomes a barrier to growth if left unchecked. The real challenge, then, is not just handling failure itself but breaking through that immediate instinct to protect ourselves and seeing it as a dead end. Imagine a restaurant concept that doesn't immediately resonate or find its audience. The first instinct may be to call it a failure, pack up, and walk away. Yet, by facing down that initial urge to quit and reframing the experience instead, essential feedback comes into play. Each setback reveals what worked, what didn't work, and where improvement can make a difference.

This shift—viewing failure as a source of vital information rather than as a verdict—is what allows us to turn setbacks into steps forward. It is this approach that defines resilient professionals; they do not see "failure" as a dead end but as an opportunity to refine their craft. This doesn't mean the setback won't sting. It will. But it reveals its value as well.

6.2 FINDING PURPOSE IN THE PAUSE

In redefining failure, I believe there is one crucial, often overlooked step: pausing purposefully before leaping into any action. There is power in that. In a society that prizes speed and productivity, the idea of pausing—especially after a setback—can feel counterintuitive. But in truth, this pause is vital. Without it, you risk missing the transformative insights that failure has to offer. This pause is a gateway to clarity, growth, and, ultimately, success—not just a break in action. Embracing this pause means facing your instinctual urge to react, rush in, fix it right away, or even cast blame. The reality is that when you pause with intention, you regain control, stepping out of the storm of emotions and into a place where perspective reigns. Once you're in that space, you see setbacks for what they really are: opportunities waiting to be unraveled.

In these moments of purposeful pause, you're building resilience by taking a moment to breathe, recalibrate, and shift your perspective. Unfortunately, many resist pausing after a setback because it's seen as a further waste of time or even a vulnerability. But that's flat out wrong! In pausing, you're not allowing a setback to define your abilities—you're letting it refine your approach. Ask yourself: What can this teach me? What is it revealing about my process, my preparation, or my mindset? What specific choices contributed to this particular outcome? Was there a gap in preparation, an oversight in planning, or a breakdown in communication? With each question, you're peeling back the layers of what happened, transforming what could be a discouraging experience into an enlightening one. Setbacks, when viewed through *the analytical eye,* become powerful teachers. They bring you back to the drawing board of your "forward focus" with newfound insights, taking you one step further on your journey—this time with much more confidence and wisdom rather than defeat and weariness.

In this intentional pause, don't just analyze—recalibrate, renew, and reinforce your commitment to growth. Ask yourself, Is this crisis unfolding because of an instinctual fear or because of a real, immediate threat? If it is an emotionally charged situation but not an urgent one, pause and reflect. If it is an operational issue—like a service crashing or a safety concern—act first, reflect later. The ability to distinguish between the two comes with practice, and it is one of the sharpest tools a professional can develop. By pausing to ask yourself the right questions, you extract the value hidden within each setback, identifying the patterns that hold you back and the actions that could propel you forward. Discover what's possible, not just what went wrong.

During my tenure as Executive Pastry Chef, we had a grand Indian wedding at the St. Regis Princeville—one of those events where no expense is spared and every detail is elevated into an art form. It was also the kind of wedding where, unfortunately, you couldn't say no to anything the guests requested. And there were over 250 of them, each one stunningly dressed, mingling beneath the rich colors and intricate floral arrangements decorating the venue.

I had met with the bride and her family months in advance for a cake tasting, where we laughed, connected, and aligned on her vision. And what a specific vision she had. She shared details about her family's heritage, the symbolic elements of the cake, and her dreams for the perfect wedding centerpiece. The cake she envisioned was intricately designed, multi-tiered, and covered with "gold feathers." I left that tasting feeling excited and confident that I could bring her vision to life. Maybe I was too eager, too certain I could pull it off. I partnered with my lead baker Chad Pacheco to bring this cake to life, and as we worked through the details (including a last-minute request for a change on the frosting), I quickly realized I had overestimated our ability to capture exactly what she envisioned. I made the decision to finish the cake and did the best we could, but the "gold feathers"—oh my goodness! They looked like a last-minute arts-and-crafts experiment gone rogue. I was so embarrassed and silently petrified.

As it was unveiled in front of her 250 guests on her wedding day, I could see the bride's horrified reaction. Her horror and dis-appointment were palpable, and I knew in that instant that I had failed to deliver the one piece of her wedding that I had promised to make perfect. I had fallen short and crushed her dreams. In the moments after, I could have easily justified the outcome, blamed the pressure, or honestly say that the last-minute change of frosting was the main reason for our failed execution. Instead, I forced myself to pause, absorb her reaction, and reflect on what went wrong. I knew this failure had come from a place of arrogance and a lack of clear communication. I had to humble myself, set aside the frustration and embarrassment, and look at the situation with an analytical eye. This pause taught me a hard truth: sometimes the best path forward is to slow down, know your limits, and assess the reality of what you can deliver rather than letting confidence and arrogance push you past your ability. That moment also taught me that sometimes failure and its impact need to be absorbed before moving on. Pausing helped me accept my limitations and reminded me that humility and reflection are just as crucial as creativity. I had failed to let the bride know months in advance that I was unable to execute her vision. My arrogance not only ruined her wedding day, it also cost several thousands of dollars of compensation.

That experience reshaped how I approach each commitment. I learned that taking a step back and embracing the pause—the pause *before* the setback—is where growth happens too. In taking space before leaping into action, I've learned to slow down, recalibrate my approach, respect the process, and prepare myself for the challenge ahead with both humility and purpose. And, in the case of those gold feathers, I realized the most powerful move would've been resisting the urge to oversell myself and my abilities from the get-go.

One way to stay grounded when making commitments is to speak from your lived experience, not what you hope to prove. If you have not led a team of ten through a high-volume service, don't say you can. Instead, acknowledge where you are, and pair that answer with your readiness to grow. Clients and interviewers are usually not looking for polished perfection; they are looking for self-awareness and realness. And when you are unsure, pause again. Say less. Ask more. That shows presence, not performative confidence. I wish I had understood this earlier—many doors might have stayed open if I had taken a breath, been real about where I stood, and trusted that honesty has its own gravity.

The strength of the analytical eye lies in its ability to detach our identity from the outcome, and that is the golden nugget here! Do not see failure as personal shortcomings but as objective feedback. In hospitality, this kind of analysis is a powerful ally. It helps us see our failures as opportunities for objective feedback, not as personal shortcomings. As you learn to cultivate this mindset, you will start to view setbacks as mile markers on a larger path toward excellence. Each pause you take, each question you ask, and each insight you gain becomes another stepping stone, helping you navigate your growth journey with clarity and a purpose-driven resolve.

6.3 PRESSING THE RESTART BUTTON

Despite the value of pausing and analyzing our setbacks, there comes a time when you wonder if you should press the restart button on a particular failure or just move on...

Starting over after a significant failure carries a unique kind of weight. Believe me, the next wedding cake I made after that disastrous gold feather fiasco was a masterpiece born from grit and humility.

Unlike our first attempt toward a goal or endeavor, which is often enthusiastic and full of boundless optimism, restarting toward that same goal after a setback is tempered by the memory of our past mistakes. We're not starting with a clean slate this time; we're beginning again with the residue of a journey that did not end as we hoped. But that's it—just the memories of what went wrong. Starting over doesn't have to be a bigger deal than it actually is. The difference now is that every step forward is informed by the hard-won insights we learned from firsthand experience.

This new beginning has a dual nature: it is both empowered by past lessons and burdened by the fear of repeating the same mistakes. This fear is an honest reaction—no one wants to relive the sting of defeat or feel the weight of disappointment again. The memories of the past failure remain, and, often, so do the questions: *What if it happens again? What if I am just not good enough?* But in choosing to start again, you confront these doubts head-on. The experience you carry with you now is invaluable. Every mistake, every setback, and every obstacle you've encountered before adds to your knowledge. Now you understand the terrain, the pitfalls, and certainly the challenges. This level of wisdom enables you to more skillfully navigate the way forward, to anticipate what might come next, and to make any necessary adjustments with a level of precision that only experience endows.

If the failure itself was not enough to bear after a setback, there's also the discomfort of self-reflection and the self-doubt that accompany it. Our perspective when beginning again captures a very human response to failure. Failure casts a long shadow, impacting more than just the task or goal itself. After a significant mistake, often we're left grappling with the dual weight of self-doubt and the shift in how others now perceive our competence. The immediate aftermath of failure can feel like stepping into a spotlight, one that tracks each move as if waiting for us to slip up again. This added scrutiny, especially from those who might have previously trusted our skills, creates a sense of unease. It's as if your capabilities have somehow downgraded overnight into something tentative or questionable. Usually, the dynamic with peers, colleagues, and/or management changes because they suddenly feel the need to micromanage your every move. Your entire skill set, it seems, is defined by a single mistake, and that makes you question yourself even more. This space is so uncomfortable and often unwarranted that you feel pressured to prove yourself all over again.

This very common situation makes pressing the restart button even harder. You find yourself at a crossroads. You're dealing with internal doubts and carrying the weight of having to rebuild trust, not only in your capabilities but in the eyes of those who are watching. You have a decision to make in this moment: You can start again, grabbing onto the opportunity to reclaim your credibility and channel your discomfort into renewed focus and precision. Or you can quit and abandon your dream, letting others' opinions of you and your own self-doubt set the tone of your next endeavors. Obviously, you know which choice I hope you make, given the foundation of growth you've already built. In choosing to begin again, though, you must find peace in navigating through that discomfort, even when others are observing you. Trying again shows everyone that a single failure does not erase years of expertise or diminish the passion and skill you bring to work on a daily basis. In fact, it can and should be the foundation of a comeback that proves to yourself and others that resilience, more than perfection, defines your journey.

In hospitality, the ability to begin again—to adapt, pivot, and try something new—is essential. Maybe you've spent months designing a menu only to find that it didn't resonate the way you hoped, or perhaps you worked tirelessly on a marketing initiative that fell flat in execution. Again, it's natural in these moments to feel doubt creeping in, wondering if it's worth it to try again, worrying that another attempt could lead to more disappointment. But here's the truth: with each restart, your foundation becomes stronger.

Pressing the restart button doesn't mean discarding everything that came before; it means finding the fortitude to approach each failure as an opportunity to reshape yourself, to rebuild your skills and perspectives with even greater resilience. This journey of reinvention, of *embracing the taste of failure*, becomes a recipe all its own. Failure becomes an ingredient you cannot avoid but one you can and must learn to work with, transforming it into something extremely valuable. This taste of failure invites you to dream even bigger, to create an even more adaptable, more capable version of yourself to present to the world.

The wedding cake disaster was a huge turning point for me. I faced the hard truth of my overconfidence and the sting of letting the bride and others down. But instead of letting that failure hold me back, I made the conscious decision to own my mistake and use it as fuel to grow. I doubled down on improving my skills, focused on the details that had tripped me up, and alongside my team, aimed to make everything in that bake shop the best we could. Each item became a testament to our shared commitment to excellence.

I refused to let that failure define me or my career; I used it to refine me instead. Rebuilding from that moment reminded me that setbacks are part of the journey, and so often the best lessons come from the toughest falls. Let's just say that the "icing on the cake" is not always a good thing. And I learned that lesson the hard way!

6.4 FALLING FORWARD: THE MINDSET

I know what you're thinking; you're expecting yet another story about some massive screw-up, some lesson I had to learn while clawing my way out of a dark moment, each misstep analyzed to build the mindset I have today. But here's the thing: I do not have any more "failures" to hand over to you. Not because I haven't hit walls or taken hard falls—believe me, I have—but because, somewhere along the way, that word lost its grip on me. "Failure" no longer holds the weight it used to. It's just a word we toss around when things do not go as planned.

The turning point for me, of course, was that wedding cake. My failure hit me so hard that day I could finally see it for what it really was: a wake-up call. From that moment on, I stopped seeing setbacks as failures, and I stopped using "failure" as a label to define my worth and career. Now, failures are nothing more than passing moments on the road to something bigger. Now, each setback is just a lesson in disguise.

This mindset brings clarity. When failure is no longer part of the equation, when the doubts and excuses that creep in with ambition fade away, what's left is a simple question: *What can I learn from this?* When this perspective becomes your go-to, your idea of success will shift. It will no longer be about rigid measures or expectations—it will become a story of growth, learning, and preparing for what's next.

After four incredible years on Kauai, some of the best in my career, I reached a major milestone: becoming Executive Chef at twenty-nine, leading the exceptional St. Regis Princeville. It was a moment I had worked hard for—a role that felt like the culmination of years of dedication. I was proud of what I had accomplished, but life has a way of testing you when you think you've settled in. A year later, another opportunity came along that I could not ignore, and I found myself at a crossroads...again.

Leaving the island for San Francisco was not a decision I took lightly. Kauai had become my home; its beauty, the community, and the rhythm of life there grounded me in a way I had not experienced before. It was there I built family-like friendships, where I felt embraced for who I was and settled for the first time in my life. Moving to the mainland meant trading that sense of peace for the hustle of the city. But the role at the St. Regis San Francisco—a Forbes 5-star property in one of the country's top food cities—was an opportunity I felt compelled to take.

San Francisco hit me harder than I expected, though. The pace of the city was overwhelming—the traffic, the crowded sidewalks, the constant noise. My daily commute, stuck in bumper-to-bumper chaos, made me long for the beaches I had left behind. And then there was the professional adjustment. The leadership style at the St. Regis San Francisco clashed with everything I valued. Decisions were made in isolation, with little regard for collaboration or the expertise I brought to the table. It felt like my voice did not matter, no matter the title I carried.

The contrast to my experience in Hawaii could not have been sharper. There, respect and community were at the heart of everything we did. At the St. Regis San Francisco, it too often felt like some people mattered more than others. The only exception to this approach was my direct supervisor, Conor Favre, a former chef who understood the nuances of our world. His approach to leadership was a breath of fresh air, but it wasn't enough to overcome the overall culture of rigidity and control.

Despite the overwhelming hardship of this move, I refused to see it as a failure. My mindset had shifted too far to allow that. I knew this chapter was teaching me something essential. I just needed to confront my values and strengthen my resolve as a leader and a chef. It was not easy. There were moments when I questioned whether I had made the right decision in leaving Kauai. But instead of running from the discomfort, I leaned into it. I reminded myself that every challenge is an opportunity to grow, even when it feels like you're being pushed against the wall. Somewhere in all the chaos, I found moments of light. Thanks to my friend Taylor Gross, I became a devoted Golden State Warriors fan, and watching their comebacks inspired me to keep going. It was a reminder that perseverance pays off, even when the odds feel stacked against you.

Looking back, my time in San Francisco was pivotal to my growth, both personal and professional. It tested me in ways I had not been tested before, but it also clarified what mattered most to me—my values, my purpose, and my direction—and I would not apologize for it. It was not a mistake; it was a lesson. It reaffirmed the importance of staying true to myself, especially when the environment didn't align with my values. The resilience that got me through this experience shaped not only the chef I became but the person I continued to grow into as well.

Because the very concept of "failure" no longer held any meaning, every goal, every challenge, and every opportunity simply became a step forward. The idea of "failing" dissolved into insignificance, leaving behind the pure pursuit of progress, growth, and discovery. And I want that same thing for you. I want your objective to not be about achieving some perfect, error-free record; I want it to be about the freedom to live, work, and create with the confidence that every experience has value, regardless of the outcome, regardless of the setbacks you face along the way.

Think about it: If you knew you could not fail, what would you do today? Would you take that bold step you've been holding back on? Would you reach for opportunities that seemed too daunting not long ago? The freedom that comes from releasing the fear of failure is transformative. When it happens, I guarantee that you'll know it! You'll be facing an open door to endless possibilities. You'll be willing to experiment, to push boundaries, and to take on challenges without an ounce of hesitation. A life without failure is a life without limits. So, what are you waiting for?

CHAPTER 7

MASTERING SKILLS: FOCUS ON THE PROGRESS

Mastering skills happens when you start focusing on your progress instead of worrying about *falling*; and that's when you really start *flying*!

Mastering skills means moving beyond just knowing the basics to truly understanding and honing your craft. It's less about collecting skills like items on a checklist and more about sticking with them long enough to make them part of you. I wish there were a black-and-white answer for what "long enough" means. But there isn't. It depends on the skill, the context, and who you are becoming in the process. What I have learned is this: mastery takes repetition, not just exposure. You must stay with it past the initial excitement, through the highs and lows, and into the quiet grind where real growth happens. Build daily rituals around the skill. Practice it deliberately. Reflect on what's improving. And refrain from chasing the next thing until this skill feels like second nature; until it shows up effortlessly in your work without you needing to think about it. That is when you know the skill has become part of who you are.

We don't achieve mastery by simply showing up and clocking in hours; we build it gradually—usually over the course of years—by accumulating knowledge, refining techniques, and, most importantly, facing our setbacks and using them to improve. There's a core difference between knowing how to do something very well and feeling how to do that thing in your very bones. Eventually, mastery becomes muscle memory, but developing it requires a certain mindset.

To master a skill is to commit yourself to the relentless pursuit of progress. But let's be real here: somewhere along the way of our lives and careers, many of us have lost a bit of that drive. As a society, we're fixated on speed and novelty. We have been told to pursue what is new and flashy, to get it fast, and to move on even faster. I have nothing against trying things out or taking a leap of faith; what I'm referring to here is the society-wide loss of drive for *depth*. Skills have become something to acquire—not master—because they look good on our resumes or LinkedIn profiles. We have conditioned ourselves to sample, taste, and check off skills from a list. There's a time and place for that, but *real* expertise? It's dismissed as too slow, too intense, too demanding. And that is where we have gone wrong. Mastery takes time and dedication to the details, something that cannot be fast-tracked and something that can feel out of place in a world that's always looking to be part of the next big thing.

The only way to rise above this noise is truly committing to mastering your craft. Obsessive dedication, perseverance, and a willingness to refine what you already know—these are the pillars of mastery. When you devote yourself to refining a skill, when you stay with it long after others have moved on, that is when you create something extraordinary. And in that depth is where professional fulfillment lives, the kind of fulfillment that cannot be found by constantly moving on from thing to thing—I guarantee you!

It is easy to overlook this process because it is both challenging and slow, and it usually takes years to reach. But when you commit to mastering your craft, you tap into a level of proficiency and expertise that sets you apart. Mastery brings with it an unmistakable confidence, precision, and quality of work. The satisfaction that comes from reaching that level of skill is profound. It is precisely this depth of mastery that opens doors and puts you in a position where you no longer need to apply for jobs; opportunities come knocking because word has gotten around about your expertise. Your next opportunity to advance, to specialize, to stand out in your field, and to inevitably achieve a reputation of excellence is then within reach. I believe that mastery and the discipline it demands is where real fulfillment comes into play. So, instead of measuring success by how many skills you can accumulate, start measuring success by how much progress you can make on the skills that matter most to your chosen craft.

I invite you to view progress as a rhythm grounded in focus, commitment, and genuine love for the craft itself, whatever that is for you. You must keep questioning, refining, and growing, not because you are unsatisfied with your abilities but because each moment of focus that you dedicate to mastery is another step toward uncovering an even deeper layer of your potential.

7.1 RITUALS OF EXCELLENCE

My experience of working at the St. Regis San Francisco, a Forbes 5-star property, demanded a nonstop pursuit of excellence and an immense responsibility. Maintaining that coveted 5-star rating was a constant and very real source of pressure, looming over every service, every meal, and every interaction.

This property was not only luxurious but also unionized, a unique factor that brought its own layers of complexity to my role as Executive Chef. In addition, this was my first time being *hired* as Executive Chef rather than being promoted to the role, as I had been in Kauai. I was responsible for all food operations, and in an establishment of this caliber, the stakes were always high. Guests both anticipated and expected perfection at every turn; after all, that's what they were paying a premium for. The entire team felt the pressure to not just meet expectations but exceed them. Working at the helm of such an operation, I learned that delivering excellence was about cultivating discipline—a ritual-ized approach to mastery, where every day and every task was a step toward refining our craft. That was exactly what I had signed up for, but that didn't make it easy.

Behind the luxurious façade was a team wrestling with the daily grind and a staff bound by union rules—and often by their own ideas of those rules. As a chef stepping into this world, I knew I needed to understand the union regulations down to the letter. I kept a copy of the collective bargaining agreement on my nightstand for the first several weeks, pouring over it late into the night to ensure I understood every clause and boundary. Ironically, I found that while many employees would confidently cite the rules, most had not actually read them. They believed they knew what was allowed but couldn't point me to where it was written. So, I used this knowledge to my advantage, not to dominate or control—okay, maybe there was a little of that—but to navigate the team, to get the best out of us while respecting the rules we had to abide by, however nuanced they might be. As I pushed my team toward excellence, there was the ever-present tension that my values did not align with the executive team's vision. Where I saw the chance to cultivate a culture of excel-lence and genuine hospitality among the culinary team, they emphasized a greater focus on procedures and metrics that, while valuable, felt disconnected from what I believed really mattered. I wanted to create something extraordinary and, most importantly, lasting—not just meet standards.

To lead in an environment like this required so much discipline and resilience, and a focused determination to refine my skills and those of the team. Every day became about ritual, about finding purpose and intention in each of our tasks, no matter how small. Everything was important—that was the essence of deliberate practice; showing up, even when the challenges seemed insurmountable, and committing to improvement, to the pursuit of mastery. After all, I would tell the team, that's what it takes to hold on to five stars with Forbes!

Early in 2016, the notification came in that we had kept the Forbes 5 stars. Not only had we maintained that pinnacle of excellence, but we now ranked among the top seventy-five hotels and resorts in the US and among the best 175 hotels and resorts worldwide. This achievement was a moment of pride for us, a nod to the relentless efforts of everyone on the team, and a testament to the rituals of excellence we had committed to every day. The 5-star rating was more than a plaque on the wall; it was our way of life, upheld by a team living and breathing excellence—a team dedicated to remaining among the best.

Achieving the level of excellence needed to become a Michelin star restaurant, a Forbes 5 star hotel, or a place known for simply serving the best food or having the best service in town doesn't happen by merely following the right steps or checking tasks off a list. Mastery is the result of an intense, sustained commitment to improvement. There are no shortcuts to mastery because mastery demands that we understand, refine, doubt, and elevate every detail of our craft. This is where the art of deliberate practice comes in. Every action becomes an opportunity to learn even more, grow even further, and close the gap between "good" and "exceptional."

Each time I needed to refine a dish, I would engage in the art of deliberate practice. I would never try to hit the standard of consistency; I would obsessively dissect every part of the process so that the end result was even more masterful. Was the scallop hitting the pan at the precise temperature to get that perfect caramelization without overcooking the center? Was the acidity of the vinaigrette lifting the dish or muting the other flavors? I would test variations, often adjusting just one variable at a time, until I found the exact thing I was after. I would run the same dish over and over again, even outside of service, pushing past the point where most would say, "That's good enough." When it looked right, when it tasted good, when nobody was complaining—that's where most chefs stopped. But for me, acceptable was not acceptable. Every dish needed to be undeniably excellent.

I remember obsessing over my grandma Alice's French onion soup; not to modernize it but to elevate it without compromising its soul. Contrary to popular opinion, the onions were not to be caramelized at all; the goal was to savor the real taste of onions, with a jammy sweetness that never crossed into dryness. I tested dozens of onions across growing seasons to find the right produce for the purpose it was meant to serve. That's why I only made onion soup during fall and winter; I simply could not find the right onions in spring and summer. I adjusted the deglazing process by seconds, revisited the balance between a perfectly and naturally colored homemade veal stock, and knew that the soup had to be baked; never just cooked on the stove. Only through very slow, radiant heat could the jammy onions and the rich veal stock fully merge, creating a kind of osmosis that simmering alone could never achieve. The flavors deepened, the texture grew round and luxurious. This was not just any onion soup. It was my grandmother Alice's, passed down with pride, perfected with care, and protected with purpose. And no matter where I've served it, it has always been a winner. Not because it was flashy, but because it was honest. Soulful. Unforgettable.

Another opportunity for mastery came in the nights when I stayed after service filleting fish in silence—sole, sea bass, trout—practicing the art with so much subtlety and délicatesse that the flesh barely moved under the knife. I wasn't required to master this skill, but I wanted to. I wanted to understand the natural lines, the tension points, the feel of the blade gliding just above the spine without resistance. Each fish taught me something new, and the repetition of doing the same thing over and over became a quiet ritual of discipline, care, and obsession. Most see filleting as a task. I saw it as a craft, my own meditation in precision.

Deliberate practice means resisting the urge to improvise too early. Mastering a skill involves repeating the same task until your hands instinctively know it. This process requires a rare kind of patience and perseverance, one that transforms ordinary tasks into a disciplined pursuit of perfection. But reaching this level means being honest with yourself about what's not working and humble enough to admit it, especially when no one else notices. Chasing inspiration won't do it; precision is what counts. When you master the details, then the inspiration shows up on its own.

The pursuit of mastery is all-consuming, because true excellence is backed by countless hours of focused effort and leaves no room for complacency. But let me be clear: achieving mastery does not necessarily mean putting in sixteen-hour days at work. The deliberate pursuit of mastery is rooted in repetition, reflection, and refinement; simply going through the motions time and time again only creates superficial results. Those who succeed at the highest level understand that their craft is built moment by moment in the repetitions, the meticulous adjustments, even the setbacks or "failures," knowing each one strengthens their foundation. That is what sets them apart.

Each intentional act of practice, or what I call *the ritual of excellence*, is an investment in mastery, and it is this investment that ultimately shapes you into who you are at the peak of your potential. Excellence is *never* an accident. It is forged in the quiet, relentless commitment to mastering your skills, when you refuse to settle for anything less than your best.

7.2 MOMENTUM IN THE MAKING

Progress over perfection. Forward focused, not flawless. Incremental gains over end destinations. This momentum—sure, steady, continual—is what forms the bridge between potential and progress. You build enough energy through your persistence and deliberate practice to sustain your own growth. When your efforts compound, you turn small wins into lasting achievements. This momentum, the fuel to mastery, *keeps* you moving forward, even when the path feels uncertain, and especially when progress is slow.

The idea of pursuing progress over perfection is one I'm still striving to internalize, and while I have made significant strides, the lesson continues to unfold. I am still learning to embrace the messy beauty of being a work in progress.

In a world driven by results, it's easy to get lost in the pursuit of perfection. Coming from the world of Michelin stars, I know this all too well. The pursuit of perfection became deeply ingrained in me at the start of my career, shaping how I worked, how I thought, and how I judged myself. While this drive helped me reach extraordinary heights and live wonderful experiences, it also left little room for grace when I didn't hit the mark. Focusing on progress, by contrast, invites me to approach growth with a different lens, one I now strongly resonate with. But to adopt this lens, I had to fall in love with the process of growth itself, seeing each step—no matter how small—as part of a larger journey.

This is a lesson I have come to understand deeply, though it did not come naturally and only hit me much later in my career. Many times, I struggled to deviate from the need to be perfect, even when it came at my own expense. In such high-stakes environments as Michelin star or Forbes 5 star kitchens, perfection often felt like the only acceptable outcome. I would too often lose sight of my steady progress, or the value of such steady progress. Instead, I would push myself—and the team—harder and harder, believing that perfection was the only measure of success worth noting. While those standards led to many incredible moments, they also created barriers and limitations to my creativity, my adaptability, and my balance.

Perfection, I realized over time, could be my guide but not my destination. Instead of chasing an unattainable ideal, I began to focus on the *progress of my perfection.* This shift didn't mean abandoning excellence; it meant redefining how I approached it. Perfection became my compass rather than a constraint, pointing me and the team toward our best work while allowing us to honor the steps it took to get there.

This mindset, while not easy to adopt, has been transformative. Progress has felt like a series of small victories. Each time I've learned something new, overcome a challenge, or found a way to improve, I felt my forward momentum. Those small moments, though often invisible to others, became the building blocks I needed to pursue mastery. In environments where expectations are high and margins for error are slim, I've learned not to let perfectionism paralyze my progress. I've learned not to let its whispers that I'll never be good enough—that I'll always be stuck in cycles of self-doubt—define me. Instead, I remember that growth happens incrementally, even if the demanding voice of perfection will always be part of the process.

Focusing on progress over perfection liberates us. It shifts our perspective from the outcome of our journey to the individual steps we take along the way. It highlights our forward momentum, which becomes an individual pursuit, a practice, and a way of both living and working. It allows us to learn, grow, and adapt without suffocating under the weight of perfection as the end goal. That is the key to mastering skills: accepting that progress is not a consolation prize—it is the fuel for everything meaningful.

This shift in perspective has transformed how I work and act as a leader. It has given me the patience to trust the process and the humility to know that I am always evolving. Perfection will always feel just out of reach, but progress is within our grasp every single day. And that, I have learned, is more than enough. Because in the end, some flawless moments in your career might define you a little, but it is the determination to keep moving forward—step by step, always in pursuit of something greater—that will make you the leader people want to follow. And as a leader, that is the best compliment you can receive.

7.3 FROM BASICS TO BRILLIANCE

I was hired at the St. Regis San Francisco for a specific mission: to collaborate with the corporate team to reimagine the closure of AME, a Michelin-starred restaurant, as an opportunity to launch a groundbreaking concept for the St. Regis brand. It was a challenge that seemed tailor-made for my ambition. Working with the Vice President of Food & Beverage Global at Starwood Hotels & Resorts was a highlight of this initiative. Alongside the Director of Food & Beverage, Conor Favre, I took on the task of piloting a new restaurant concept—one that would become the flagship for St. Regis properties worldwide if successful. It was an exhilarating yet intimidating challenge and one I leapt into headfirst, fully determined to make it work.

Months of meticulous work followed. My collaborators and I painstakingly considered every detail—menu creation, beverage pairings, interior design, furniture, plateware, glassware—the list was endless. Every tasting, debate, and brainstorming session was fueled by our shared desire to create something extraordinary. I loved the process, despite the inevitable frustrations that came with so many voices involved. At times, it felt like there were too many hands in the pot, too many differing opinions, and this tested my leadership in ways I hadn't experienced before. Still, the goal remained clear: to bring a concept to life that would redefine expectations and solidify my place as an Executive Chef to take note of.

Then came the first twist of 2016. AME was closing for good after a month-to-month collaboration so we could get ready to open. The moment we got the news, I felt heat rise in my chest. All our strategy, alignment, and refinement in the garbage. Just like that. I glanced at Conor, who looked just as stunned. "This is it," he said. "Seventy-two hours. We need a full pivot." That was all the time they gave us to completely reimagine the concept.

I didn't answer at first. I laughed; not because it was funny, but because the situation felt surreal. I just stared ahead, breathing through the frustration. "Seriously?" I finally muttered. "After everything?"

My frustration was real, but so was the deadline. There was no time to spiral. We gathered the core team in the back kitchen; tight space, sharp energy. I kept the delivery short and clear. "The concept's dead. New corporate's moving in a different direction. We have three days to recreate ourselves. We are shifting to a grill-focused concept." There was a beat of silence, then push-back. A few groans. One sous-chef muttered something under his breath. Another cook shook his head and said, "That is insane."

"It is," I replied. "But we are doing it anyway. And I need everyone's help to make it happen." Some were too vocal, too resistant. But we only had three days to design a brand-new concept, train the team on that concept, adjust the furniture and layouts, and deliver something worthy of the St. Regis name.

Over the course of those three days, I had to lean on the

principles that had carried me this far. We made quick decisions and moved forward with a motivated but confused crew. Within a few hours, we were sketching a new menu: prime cuts from Snake River Farms and Creekstone, composed appetizers we could execute under pressure, and refined desserts with their own character.

That kitchen was running on adrenaline. We rewrote prep sheets, retrained the team, called in vendors at odd hours. The ovens ran nonstop, we were fatigued, and tempers flared. But somehow, it all moved forward. And through the chaos, there was also focus. We did not just react; we rebuilt with intention, with urgency, and, most of all, with a lot of pride.

On opening day, we were as ready as we could be, given the mere seventy-two hours we'd been given to redesign everything. Our first service was a trial by fire, as expected. We made mistakes, but the team rallied. We met every problem with a solution and every setback with persistence. By the end of the night, we'd pulled off what many thought was impossible. It wasn't perfect by any means, but it was a triumph in its own right. And just as we found our footing with the new grill concept, a second wave of uncertainty struck.

In September 2016, Starwood Hotels & Resorts merged with Marriott International, sending ripples through the company and shaking the foundations of our upcoming project. Delays, reapprovals, and a new chain of decision-makers disrupted the momentum we had built. The merger did not just alter processes;

it fundamentally changed the culture of the organization, shifting priorities and casting doubt on the project's future. It felt like we were being robbed of the brand's identity. Still, we adjusted, determined to see the vision through.

In December, an even greater disruption arrived: the ownership of the St. Regis San Francisco changed hands, adding yet another layer of complexity to an already complex project. Everything we had meticulously planned came under scrutiny. The green light we were waiting for felt increasingly out of reach, replaced by doubts and further corporate delays. The emotional toll was undeniable—frustration, uncertainty once more, and anger. All of it simmered just beneath the surface of our team. But as a leader, I knew we couldn't afford to dwell on those feelings. I needed to approach this new challenge with flexibility, not rigidity.

I was still finding my footing as an Executive Chef, but the countless hours I'd spent refining my skills—understanding flavor profiles, executing with precision, and managing teams under pressure—became the foundation that steadied me when everything else was shaky. This depth of knowledge and the discipline I'd gained from years of deliberate practice carried me through that challenge. I had the confidence to lead, the adaptability to pivot, and the resilience to push through. Without that solid foundation, this moment might have broken me. Instead, it became a defining milestone in my career.

This experience taught me that mastery begins when

competence ends. Once we have learned the fundamentals and built a solid foundation, the real work of mastery reveals itself, not as an endpoint we've reached but as a transformation we've undergone. Mastery moves us from basics to brilliance—that is the transformative journey of mastering our craft, and it's neither an easy one nor a short one.

Mastery requires patience, resilience, and a willingness to both embrace and live in discomfort. This mindset is not automatic; it must be cultivated, *daily*. It requires discipline. Not the kind that feels forced, but the kind that becomes a part of who you are. It requires that we show up and repeat the same tasks with focus and purpose until they become second nature. It requires living in the tension between striving for perfection and accepting that perfection is unattainable.

Real transformation lies in this tension. It lies in the gap between perfection and progress, where the small, overlooked details form the building blocks of momentum; where the consistent effort, intention, and impact you put toward your craft form a bridge between potential and progress. That's when the basics transform into brilliance, and the ordinary turns into the exceptional. That is how mastery evolves.

CHAPTER 8

ATTENTION TO DETAIL: FINDING MEANING TO FULFILLMENT

It's time to bring our focus inward—into the heart of what *relentless growth* is all about: finding fulfillment. This has been the invisible thread running through every chapter, every concept, and every story. But fulfillment is not a singular moment of arrival or a trophy we hang on the wall. It is so much deeper than that. It is the alignment of who you are with the life you are building. In these final chapters, we'll connect the dots between the work you have done, the lessons you've learned, and the career you are creating, all of which cultivate fulfillment. This is where it all comes together—the growth, the grit, and the meaning behind it all.

First things first, let's make something clear: fulfillment *is* a feeling. It's a quiet pulse of satisfaction, deeply personal yet profoundly universal. It has nothing to do with the rush of applause or the glitter of accolades. It is the far more subtle sense that what you are doing *matters*. And the most surprising thing? Fulfillment often finds you when you're not looking for it. Chasing it down won't work; it's something you stumble on when you are immersed in the moment. It sneaks up in the rhythm of deliberate action, in the flow of doing your best work, and in the stillness that follows after you have given your all to something. Fulfillment doesn't announce itself. It settles in, grounding you with a sense of purpose that feels unshakable. But you must stay present in the moment long enough to notice the subtle connections weaving through your work.

Fulfillment is born in the details. It is in the curve of a perfectly folded napkin and the alignment of tables in the restaurant. It's in the timing of a joke that lifts up the team during a tough pre-shift, or in the quiet decision to stay five minutes longer to finish something right instead of running off to a smoke break. These details create a mosaic of meaning, each one linking your work to a greater sense of who you are and what you stand for.

When you pay attention to these important moments, fulfillment reveals itself as an ongoing experience. The beauty of it is that it asks nothing from you, except to show up—fully, genuinely, and with intention. The more you lean into the work itself, the more fulfillment finds you. It teaches you that the smallest details, the quietest moments, and the unnoticed efforts often hold the greatest meaning. It was always there, waiting for you to see it. When you home in on these details, you unleash their transformative power—because it's within their subtle connections that both your work and your sense of purpose take shape. You must embrace the seemingly minor, easily overlooked moments along your journey of growth and recognize their profound role in shaping your craft and your character. Once you start noticing these moments, fulfillment stops being so elusive and instead becomes an integral, steady presence, anchoring you with meaning and driving you toward your best self.

8.1 THE SILENT ADVANTAGE

When I left San Francisco, something was beginning to shift within me. I could not fully articulate it at the time, but it was there: quiet, persistent, unsettling. The city had been a proving ground, a place where I tested every ounce of my discipline, drive, and leadership. I had given everything I had to the St. Regis brand: early mornings, late nights, pressure absorbed without complaint. But as the Marriott merger took full effect, something changed. The brand I had once been fiercely loyal to started blurring into something else. Meetings became more about compliance than creativity. Approval processes tripled. Leaders I respected quietly exited. Corporate memos began replacing real conversations. And slowly, spreadsheets squeezed out the human part of hospitality—the part I had devoted my life to.

Deep down, I had hoped that St. Regis would show some loyalty in return for all the years I gave. But what was I expecting? It was a corporation after all, not a family. And yet, I could not ignore how deeply that truth cut. I had exhausted myself aiming for perfection inside of a machine, where hitting numbers mattered more than developing people or craft. I was young, still stubborn, and, at times, unfiltered. I stood up for what I believed in, sometimes too loudly. I would call out contradictions in leadership meetings. I challenged decisions I felt betrayed the soul of the brand. I did not play the game, and I paid for that.

When I was suddenly placed on a performance improvement plan, it felt less like getting feedback and more like receiving a quiet ultimatum. There were no prior conversations. No warnings. Just a scheduled meeting, a cold document, and a hollow statement: "We are here to support your success." But "success" wasn't about performance. It was about principles. And everyone in the room knew it. I was being asked to conform, to silence the parts of me that no longer fit neatly inside their new system. And that more than anything signaled it was time for me to go.

The abruptness of it all stung; but it also confirmed what had been quietly bothering me for some time. I had chosen to stand up for beliefs I considered nonnegotiable: fairness, integrity, and leadership that prioritized people over optics. My values and theirs were misaligned.

It was not just this misalignment that bothered me, it was also the realization that the system I loved, enjoyed, and had worked within for quite some time did not reward those who dared to question or challenge the status quo. A deeper shift was beginning to take hold in me too; the weight I had once placed on external achievements was waning. As we were emerging from the chaos of launching a new concept and navigating the merger while trying to keep the standard intact, I simply could not ignore it anymore. The shift wasn't loud or dramatic; just a slow, persistent discomfort with the idea that stars, titles, and accolades were the highest markers of success. The hard truth was clear now: external benchmarks like Forbes stars, titles, and accolades were just that—external.

While I genuinely enjoyed the accolades I'd received, I still felt a conflict within me. My career as it was did not fully align with the deeper sense of purpose I was beginning to crave, one rooted in authenticity, values, and principles worth fighting for. That realization marked the start of a transformation, one where I started to measure success on my own terms rather than someone else's metrics.

Then a deeper realization came: the gap between the corporate way of thinking and my own values was not just wide, it was unbridgeable. The corporate world demanded compliance, meeting metrics, and sticking to rigid structures, while I craved creativity, authenticity, and humanity. I tried so hard to align myself with the corporate way of thinking, but I could no longer force myself into that mold. Leaving my position at the St. Regis was not just about stepping away from a job or a city; it meant stepping into myself, unapologetically. I began to find meaning not in the relentless grind but in the intention behind my work. I realized that success was not just about numbers or accolades but about the overall integrity I brought to each task and every decision, about staying true to what mattered most to me—the craft, the people, and the journey of constant growth.

This inner change became the start of my journey to fulfillment. And I realized it was not about what I was leaving behind but what I was moving toward. That shift entailed a deeply personal reorientation of how I approached my work, my relationships, and myself. And in that clarity, I found something the corporate world could not offer me anymore: meaning.

Fulfillment begins with awareness, and awareness is all about attention. Attention to detail starts with observing your environment, your work, and, most importantly, yourself. This is not a passive act; it is an active commitment to seeing what others overlook. The smallest things often matter most. Observations reveal opportunities, tiny cracks where improvement can seep through, shaping both the outcome of a task and the quality of the journey along the way. Details are *never* insignificant. They form the foundation of trust, excellence, and growth. A misaligned garnish on a plate, a poorly worded email, or an overlooked comment in a meeting can ripple outward, affecting outcomes in ways that seem disproportionate to their size. Conversely, the ability to notice, *think*, and address such details enhances not just the immediate task but also your reputation and presence in your work.

In the kitchen, I trained myself to read the room without interrupting it. I would study how cooks set up their stations—the way they pressed their uniforms, how they arranged their mise en place, whether their knives were wiped down or still dirty from the morning prep. I watched how they moved, how often they checked the clock or their phone, whether they cleaned as they worked or waited until they were behind. Over time, I became known for this silent observation. I was always watching, and the kitchen knew it. I didn't need to raise my voice. My presence alone made people nervous. Cooks used to say they could feel when I was behind them, even if I hadn't said a word. That pressure raised the standard. It made them better. And it kept me sharp too. Because when you train yourself to see what others miss, you start to lead before you ever speak. There's a quiet fulfillment in that—knowing your impact doesn't come from volume but from vision.

The art of observation is the entry point to deeper understanding. Through this awareness, fulfillment stops being a vague concept and becomes an intentional action. When you pair your awareness with action—correcting a misstep, offering a thoughtful solution, finding a way to make something better—your attention to detail becomes transformative.

Acting on what you notice demonstrates accountability and

reinforces a culture where excellence is not the exception but the expectation.

As you refine this ability to observe and then act on what you observe, fulfillment shifts from an elusive goal to something intrinsic to the work itself. The process of intentionally seeing, improving, and striving becomes a source of pride and purpose. Work is no longer just a task to complete; it is an expression of your dedication and identity. The question always remains: Are you looking closely enough? And, perhaps more importantly, what will you do with what you see?

8.2 STANDING AT THE INTERSECTION

There is a common belief that chefs fall prey to when searching for meaning and fulfillment: paying attention to details requires obsessive precision, nothing less. We think that every detail demands absolute perfection, because that is what we do. But there's a difference between presence and precision. **Presence fuels the why, precision delivers the how.**

What does this mean? In environments where excellence is nonnegotiable, precision promises control and mastery. Paying attention to detail with absolute precision elevates a craft from good to great. This is celebrated as a cornerstone of professionalism, a mark of distinction. But precision comes at a cost; when it becomes your sole focus, you risk severing the connection between you and the purpose of your work. Precision demands discipline, technical skill, and a whole lot of attention. Don't get me wrong, these are all invaluable pursuits; but when precision becomes your sole obsession, it tends to create a barrier to fulfillment rather than a bridge.

I know this all too well and sometimes still find myself in that headspace. Course correcting requires an ongoing commitment to self-reflection and self-assessment, otherwise the pursuit of perfection will narrow your vision and have you fixating on the minutiae of your work while neglecting the bigger picture. Over time, this approach will make your work primarily a mechanical endeavor, draining from it the sense of meaning and connection that once motivated you. The result? You deliver something technically flawless but emotionally flat, a work that might impress but does not inspire.

Think of a dish plated with precision but not presence. It will look flawless, but it will also lack soul. Now imagine the same dish, plated by someone who is fully present, someone who pours their care and personality into the process. It feels alive—it has a story, a voice, and a purpose. This is the main difference between work that is technically impressive and work that resonates.

Delivering something technically flawless but emotionally flat is one of the greatest traps for professionals striving for excellence. On the surface, perfection might seem like the ultimate goal—it wows, satisfies, and earns approval. But over time, work that prioritizes technical mastery over emotional connection begins to lose its impact. It becomes predictable, rigid, or even forgettable. For those on the receiving end, it feels polished yet distant, failing to spark the kind of engagement or emotion that truly memorable work inspires. For the creator, focusing on perfection alone fosters a sense of detachment from the work, as the joy of creation gives way to a mechanical pursuit of approval. That is the ultimate danger of aiming solely for precision—sacrificing the *humanity* that makes our work meaningful.

Precision and presence might seem like opposites, but they're really two sides of the same coin. Precision entails skill, consistency, and excellence, while presence anchors you in the purpose behind why you're pursuing skill, consistency, and excellence. Neither precision nor purpose can truly thrive without the other. The world's most esteemed restaurants and hotels—those graced with three Michelin stars or awarded five stars by Forbes—understand this balance intimately. They recognize that while precision is essential, it is the collision of precision and presence that creates an unforgettable experience. These establishments do not just deliver flawless service or exquisite dishes; they infuse each interaction, each plate, with a sense of purpose and emotion—this is what sets them apart. Again, presence is not about abandoning precision; it is about tuning in to your craft as a series of moments to inhabit and infuse with purpose, not just a series of tasks to flawlessly complete.

Remember, precision refines, but presence elevates. Think of a three-star Michelin restaurant where every dish is executed with technical perfection. That alone is notable, but it is the presence of the chef and the team—their passion, focus, and care—that turns a meal into a lasting memory. The same holds true in five-star hotels and resorts. Impeccable standards are expected, but it is the warmth of the welcome, the attention to unspoken needs, and the genuine connection that make the stay unforgettable. This is where precision and presence collide; this is where the magic happens.

Achieving this balance is not easy. The daily grind of excellence—tight deadlines, demanding standards, and constant scrutiny—often tips the scale toward precision. Success metrics and stakeholder expectations pull hospitality workers into outcome obsession. In these environments, presence can feel like a luxury. But neglecting it comes at the cost of our work losing its soul. The challenge is knowing when precision is overpowering everything else, and choosing to reclaim presence. The best establishments do this intentionally. They build presence into their culture, training not just for skill but for connection.

This partnership between precision and presence sustains passion. And it's where fulfillment lives too. It is where a dish becomes iconic, a stay becomes a story, and a guest becomes an advocate. I believe this interplay is where true artistry lives. Precision grounds you. Presence lets you soar. Together, they do not just create excellence; they create your legacy.

8.3 DAILY PRACTICES, QUIET REWARDS

The world of luxury, fine dining, and high-pressure accolades has been the backdrop of my journey. But professional fulfillment is not confined to Michelin stars, Forbes 5-star ratings, or even the pursuit of perfection. For years, I thought it was. I chased every benchmark and every accolade, believing they would lead me to my deeper sense of purpose. But over time, I came to realize that true fulfillment is not found in the recognition—it is always found in the process. I share my experiences not because they are the only way to achieve personal and professional growth, but because they shaped me and taught me the power of a growth mindset. We must each follow our own paths to fulfillment, which can be found anywhere that aligns with who we are and what we value. And, of course, by embracing the mindset that every step of the journey we're on matters—we just have to pay attention.

There's a subtle but transformative difference between "getting the job done" and "doing it well." And I believe fulfillment lives within this subtlety. "Getting the job done" is a transactional approach—you complete a task, check a box, and move on to the next thing. It is often driven by urgency, efficiency, or a desire to finish something as quickly as possible. While there is nothing inherently wrong with efficiency, it leaves little room for pride, purpose, or progress. "Doing it well," on the other hand, is an intentional approach. It is not just about finishing a job—but about *how* you finish that job. It means bringing focus, care, and effort to the task at hand, no matter how small.

Why is this difference so important? Because "getting the job done" is *forgettable*—doing tasks this way leaves little to no trace of growth or impact. But "doing it well" is *meaningful*—it builds trust in your abilities and pride in your work, and it creates habits that foster excellence. Every time you *choose* to do something well instead of merely checking off a to-do list, you are *choosing* to reinforce who you are and who you are becoming. You are declaring your standards to yourself and the world.

In 2017, I left San Francisco and found myself in Sedona, Arizona, for the next step of my journey. Sedona felt like stepping into a completely different rhythm of life, one shaped by nature rather than schedules. The red rocks of Sedona are eye-catching, not just because they are beautiful but because they seem to carry a quiet strength, like they have seen it all and just keep standing. It is easy to feel a sense of perspective when surrounded by that kind of permanence. I remember the very first time I saw them. Before I had gotten the job, I arrived late at night for my Executive Chef tasting. When I woke up, there they were, surrounding me with such breathtaking beauty that I felt it right down to my core. I felt immediately connected to the place.

When I relocated to Sedona—after landing the job of course—it felt like starting with a clean slate. I had left the rush of the city and all its distractions. The Sedona air had a clarity to it, reminding me to breathe differently, to breathe deeper. Of course, at 4,500 feet above sea level, I definitely *had* to take deeper breaths. The mornings were quiet, the kind of quiet that lets you hear your own thoughts, and the evenings were luxurious and long, always with enough time to reflect. This was not just a new chapter—it was a different kind of story altogether. One with nature at the very center of it. Living there slowed me down, not in a way that felt like losing momentum, but in a way that made me feel more deliberate, more present. Sedona taught me to appreciate that pace, to find value in stepping back, and to recognize that new beginnings can arrive softly. I felt a sense of déjà vu, like I was back in the islands, away from everything.

At the time, I was being scouted by the ownership team of a property in town for a position that was impossible to ignore. L'Auberge de Sedona, one of the most iconic properties in the area, had noticed me. More than that, they noticed everything I had sought to develop over the course of my career: my reputation for discipline, my obsession with precision, and my focus on the daily rituals of excellence. These quiet efforts had steadily built my reputation over the years, and now they were opening a door I hadn't expected. I'm sure my future wife and unofficial PR manager, Kristin, who worked for L'Auberge de Sedona, also played a role in sparking interest and putting my name into the conversation, so I'll give her some credit too.

L'Auberge de Sedona is a place where Sedona's magic comes alive. Perched on the banks of Oak Creek, surrounded by towering trees and dappled sunlight, it offers a rare blend of rustic, intimate charm and refined luxury. There, nature and hospitality meet seamlessly, inviting guests into an experience that feels deeply personal. The job opportunity they were scouting me for was to lead as their Executive Chef *and* to take on the role of Director of Food & Beverage, overseeing Orchards Inn as well with 89Agave Cantina, the best Mexican restaurant in town. If I landed these roles, it would not just be a step forward in my career, it would be a leap into a position of trust and responsibility that perfectly aligned with the leader I aspired to be.

What made this moment significant beyond the opportunity itself was a quiet realization: the daily practices and the small, deliberate actions I had committed to throughout my career had led me there. I had built a foundation of consistency and excellence, and now I was standing firmly on what I'd built. Early mornings spent planning every detail of service, thousands of hours grinding for my own growth, the quiet moments of reflecting on what went well and what didn't, my relentless pursuit of betterment. These practices, unnoticed by most, formed the very essence of my current fulfillment and my still unfolding career.

When L'Auberge de Sedona came calling, I was working at the Enchantment Resort. Even though I had only been on the job six months, I had encountered frustrations that were hard for me to ignore. I had been hired to bring about change, yet management met every one of my attempted steps forward with resistance. When I arrived at L'Auberge de Sedona, the contrast could not have been clearer. There, I was given the freedom to lead, to make decisions that would benefit the property, and to channel my experience into something meaningful. Trust was the currency of our exchange, and it was invigorating. My daily rituals of precision and presence found a home there, and they became the cornerstone of what I would build.

I applied myself fully at L'Auberge de Sedona, not for the accolades but for the quiet rewards that came from progress and fulfillment. I had perfected the art of being present, of noticing the small details that could elevate a guest's experience or strengthen a team member's performance. One thing was for sure, I knew how to build a badass team, so I started right away. The work was as much about building something special as it was about refining myself in the process. Word on the street about my arrival at L'Auberge de Sedona traveled fast, and several team members from the Enchantment Resort jumped ship to join me on my new adventure. It felt great that after just six months together, my former team members wanted to remain a part of my journey—though I imagine the Enchantment Resort might have felt a little less enchanted with me by the end.

Sedona had a way of grounding me while simultaneously lifting me higher. At L'Auberge de Sedona, I found a place that mirrored the qualities I valued. We aligned in both purpose and practice, trust and autonomy. The fulfillment I experienced there was not in the title I held or the accolades I received—I was fully and obsessively in love with the process itself, in the daily commitment to excellence we shared and the quiet rewards that followed. This chapter of my journey reinforced a truth I had long understood: success is not a single destination. It is progression, an accumulation of small but powerful efforts, deliberate actions, and daily practices; the rewards of this journey may not always be visible to others, but they resonate deeply within each one of us committed to growth.

When we build habits of excellence, these habits compound, creating momentum that carries us through the inevitable challenges within any career and propels us toward the goals we hold close to our hearts. If there is one takeaway from this chapter that I want you to remember, it is this: care about the work in front of you, no matter how small it seems. Show up for the process. Do it well because it matters—not to anyone else, but to you. That is where you'll find fulfillment, and it is something you can create every day.

8.4 THE BUILDING BLOCKS OF PURPOSE

Professional fulfillment is the driving force behind a meaningful work life. I unapologetically stand by this statement because I have lived it—and there is no substitute for the passion it brings. It's what keeps my energy alive and my ambition moving forward. It's what fuels my drive to grow, to learn, and to create something meaningful—not just for myself but for the people I work with and the impact I want to leave behind. Because I have prioritized professional fulfillment, I wake up every day with a purpose, knowing that the work I do matters, that it challenges me to be better, and that I'm *living* my life, not simply *existing* in it.

The alternative? That's a reality I can't accept. The average person between the ages of twenty and sixty-five spends 23 percent of their life working, which is about 90,000 hours. If you work in hospitality, though, you're probably laughing at these numbers. "Only 23 percent? Must be nice to work part time!" But imagine going through your entire career, be it 23 percent of your time or 50, just waiting for the day you can retire, taking no real joy in the work you do. Think about it—waking up every morning, dreading the hours ahead, feeling no connection to your efforts. Work becomes a lifeless routine, the days blurring together, until all you're left with is the hope of some distant freedom years down the line. To me, that is not living, that is existing.

In 2018, I was a few weeks into a role at L'Auberge de Sedona that would become one of the most challenging and rewarding of my career. Sedona's charm came with its own set of challenges. For one, the labor market was painfully small. The town's distance from major cities meant a limited pool of talent, and the reputation I had inherited—a combination of broken trust and toxic workplace culture in Food & Beverage—made it even harder to attract the kind of team I needed to elevate the experience. In hospitality, your people are everything. You can't deliver world-class service without them, and in Sedona, we had to attract, retain, and nurture great employees at all costs.

At L'Auberge, the culinary crown jewel was Cress on Oak Creek, an intimate restaurant along the water. Known for its riverside setting and its dedication to seasonal, concept-driven, and locally inspired cuisine, it offered a blend of elegance and authenticity that had been lost in the turbulence of years prior. Rebuilding the food & beverage department entailed far more than creating new dishes to put on the menu. I had to reignite pride in the experience of dining there, and, more importantly, working there. This endeavor was all-consuming, but I loved it. I thrived in it. There was so much to do: rebuild trust, fix broken processes, and craft a new vision for what we could achieve.

It was hard, yes, but it was also fulfilling in a way that few things are in life. I had the vision. I knew what needed to happen to transform the department and bring it back to its full potential, and that meant being there—constantly. Countless hours passed as I dove headfirst into every aspect of the operation, from hiring and training to refining the guest experience. I needed help, so I called some of my former chefs—the best ones I've ever had—to come work with me on the project, and they answered the call. John Gapasin, my executive sous chef, was known for always being tired but showing up anyway, always there and finishing strong. Miranda Ulrich, my pastry lead, moved with a calm, collected grace that never wavered: solid, steady, and unshaken no matter how wild service got. And Yannick "Neek" Law, my *chef de cuisine*, could keep everything focused and in check no matter what.

Building something special became my mission. I focused not only on attracting talent but on creating an environment where people wanted to stay—a culture of trust, respect, and collaboration. Piece by piece, I put together one of the best teams I've ever had the honor to lead. In time, the team didn't just meet expectations; they exceeded them. Retention became a nonissue, engagement levels soared, and together we delivered excellence— word of which traveled through Sedona and beyond. Over time, we were finally able to put our destination back on the map.

This work was not just a job; it was a calling, and I took immense joy in the process. It was deeply fulfilling to watch the team come together despite the odds and adversities, to see their pride in what we had built, knowing that we had created something truly exceptional. The hours I put in never felt like a burden because the joy of building something truly special far outweighed the sacrifice. L'Auberge de Sedona became my testament to what's possible when you fully commit yourself to a vision. It was one of the hardest positions I've held, but it shaped me in ways I will forever be grateful for. It reminded me that, while the road to professional fulfillment is never easy, it is worth every step.

Now, if you've made it this far in the book, it's reasonable to assume that you are no longer just curious about growth and fulfillment—you are committed to them. Committed to personal growth, regardless of where you find yourself in your career. Committed to figuring out what professional fulfillment looks like for you and how to make it a reality. That says something about your mindset, about your willingness to go beyond the surface and dive into what truly matters. It is proof that you are ready to take the steps necessary to bring purpose and meaning into your work. It's also reasonable to assume that, by now, you know professional fulfillment does not happen by chance. It is built brick by brick with the building blocks of purpose: knowing your "why," staying connected to it, and making consistent, intentional choices that align your work with your values, your precision with presence, and your "why" with your "how."

Without professional fulfillment, work becomes a hollow means to an end—a paycheck, a title, or a way to pass time. But at what cost? The cost is your spirit, your wasted potential, and the joy you could have had in building something truly remarkable. Working without fulfillment means settling for mediocrity and staying within comfort zones that do not challenge or excite you. Looked at this way, professional fulfillment is not just a goal—it is a necessity. It's what makes the late nights and hard work worth it. It turns a job into a calling and a career into a legacy. And I wholeheartedly believe you deserve to feel that level of joy in what you do. Settling for anything less is not just a missed opportunity—it is a life not fully lived.

CHAPTER 9
UNIQUE MINDSET: ADOPT THE CHANGE

Let's take a moment to pause and reflect on the journey we've traveled together through the first eight chapters of this book. This is *your* time—your chance to breathe, absorb, and process the perspectives that have shifted and the potential that has awakened inside you. Take this moment to recognize how far you've come and to prepare yourself for what's ahead. What has shifted for you? What is stirring inside? The work does not stop here; it is just beginning. Let's dig deeper, push harder, and move forward with intention.

Remember, growth is not a single event or a destination. It is a way of moving through your professional life with purpose and resilience. You've already taken the critical steps of defining a vision by staying curious to what feels alive within you, building a roadmap toward that vision (your forward focus with intention), embracing the inevitable uncertainty of the journey, and thriving under the pressure of your growing momentum. Now it's time to bring everything together. This chapter will help you synthesize the lessons you've learned from your journey thus far as you step fully into a mindset that not only accepts change but thrives on it. Your newly adopted growth mindset shapes how you interact with the world, how you view your experiences, and how you utilize the tools you've developed along the way. This is the moment of transformation—where your pursuit of relentless growth becomes a deeply personal, internalized force.

At its core, this transformation demands consistency, a whole lot of patience, and an obsessive commitment to self-awareness. Transformation doesn't happen when you follow someone else's definition of success; it happens when you define what growth means to you personally, professionally, and holistically. It happens when you turn your aspirations into intentional actions—when the work you've done so far becomes ingrained in your character, not as a checklist of accomplishments but as a way of life. Growth, after all, is less about reaching a pinnacle and more about finding joy and meaning in the climb itself, as it requires both the humility to accept where you are today and the courage to reach for more tomorrow. If you wake up happy and fulfilled, balancing your ambition with your ability to adapt, you have redefined your idea of success and you are living and breathing the philosophy of relentless growth.

It is finally time for you to cross the threshold of transformation and step fully into the version of yourself that has been waiting all along. And I promise you, it was always there!

9.1 BREAKING FREE: YOUR STORY, YOUR GROWTH

This is your story! You decide how it is written. You and only you. Breaking free of others' narratives and beliefs about you and your life means letting go of what no longer serves you and owning every part of *your* journey. Growth starts when you take back control of your story and move forward, fully yourself.

What you can control—your reactions, your focus, your energy—becomes your anchor. You embrace challenges with newfound poise, knowing that the real strength of leadership does not come from shouting above the noise but from listening, adapting, and leading with clarity.

Back in the red rocks of northern Arizona at L'Auberge de Sedona, we learned that our management company was being acquired by Hyatt Hotels Corporation. It was the end of 2018 and, it seemed, the end of an era. For any hospitality team, a flag change represents a monumental shift. But for us, this news carried even more weight—it marked the third general manager for the resort in less than eighteen months and the second management company transition in just over a year. The ripple effect of yet another change was palpable within the team—instability and apprehension stirred across the property.

A flag change entails far more than a name swap and a new logo. It is a complete overhaul of standards, systems, and often, culture. There are new core values to learn and guiding principles to uphold. New software tools replace familiar ones, forcing employees to adapt once again and leaders to attend even more training sessions to get acclimated with new procedures. Processes as simple as clocking in or submitting reports can suddenly become unfamiliar hurdles.

I remember gathering the teams—the restaurant staff and kitchen crew—to break the news personally. There was silence at first, the kind that settles in when people hear what they fear. Faces were tight with uncertainty. Some asked what this meant for their roles, others didn't say much at all. But the question I got more than once was the same: "Are you leaving?" That was what they really wanted to know. And when I told them I was not going anywhere, I could feel the shift in the room. Shoulders relaxed. Eyes lifted. There was no celebration, but there was a quiet sense of relief. For them, my presence meant continuity. It meant that whatever changes were coming, someone they trusted would be there to navigate them with them. That moment reminded me that leadership doesn't mean having all the answers; it means giving people something to hold onto when everything else feels uncertain.

For some, the weight of these changes was still compounded

by a sense of lingering uncertainty. Would the new company retain all the existing staff? What expectations would they bring with a new corporate team? Would the values and culture that made L'Auberge de Sedona unique be preserved—or altered? And if altered, how much?

There was only so much we could do to ensure the acquisition did not affect the guest experience, but the transition was more than stressful; it disrupted the heart of what made the resort so special at the time. Employees at every level felt the strain. Many worried about job security, while others struggled to find their footing amid so much disruption in their work life. With the revolving door of general managers, there was little sense of continuity or direction. The sheer scale of what we faced—new standards, new leadership, new expectations from new bosses— was overwhelming to both the staff and leadership team.

Leadership in times of transition entails a fair amount of pretending that everything is fine. We had to navigate discomfort and uncertainty with a steady hand, reassuring our team daily while quietly managing our own doubts about the future. For me, the challenges of this merger tested every ounce of my past experiences and perspective. But I knew from years in the industry that such changes, as daunting as they seemed, did not have to define us. With the right mindset—a growth mindset—this moment became an opportunity to demonstrate resilience and adaptability as a team.

The priority was clear for leadership at the top: ensure that the guest experience and daily operations remain unaffected. The guests at L'Auberge de Sedona had no idea about the management company transition happening behind the scenes, and it was our job to keep it that way. At the same time, I had to be present for my team, acknowledging their fears while encouraging them to focus on what they could control. There were moments when anxiety felt like the undercurrent of every service, every hallway conversation. Staff members, already fatigued and frustrated by the previous year's change, had to undergo more training, learn unfamiliar systems, and adapt to a new corporate culture. In this environment, maintaining our calm and composure became our greatest tools. The ones who began to thrive were those who embraced the discomfort, leaning into the uncertainty of the transition with a growth mindset instead of resisting it.

As Director of Food & Beverage, the responsibility of ensuring stability for the team fell heavily on my shoulders. My growth mindset anchored me during this time, reminding me that change, no matter how chaotic, could be a catalyst for improvement. Looking back, this acquisition by Hyatt Hotels Corporation was more than just a corporate event to navigate through; it was, for many, a crucible, testing both our resilience and our patience. For me, it was an impactful reminder of what true leadership demands in moments of uncertainty: to stay calm when everything around you is shifting, and to guide the team with clarity, purpose, and a little dose of humor. It is wild to think that just a few weeks later, during an ownership visit, we secretly learned—spoiler alert!—they were not interested in having Hyatt Hotels Corporation manage the resort. Which meant *another* change was on the horizon. But the question remained: When?

Sometimes, out of nowhere, you receive an invitation—wanted or not—to take ownership of your story and write the next chapter with boldness, curiosity, and a complete refusal to stay small. Fixed mindsets thrive on certainty. They crave predictability and control, weaving together a narrative that suggests growth is linear, predefined, and safe. But growth, *your* growth, never follows a straight line, and the rules that dictate your potential are not fixed; they are flexible, ready to be reshaped by your choices.

What if the limits you see are not real? What if the ceiling above you is built with assumptions, not facts? So much of what holds us back is not the world around us—it is the story we tell ourselves about what is possible. Rewriting the rules of our potential and breaking free from the limits holding us back begins with one radical question: *What is stopping you?* Don't ask yourself this question in a judgmental way; ask it as an invitation to examine the forces at play, such as fear, self-doubt, societal expectations, pressure, or even the comfort of routine. Ask yourself if those limits serve you or if they are constructs you have outgrown. Your story is not confined to a singular path, nor is your growth tied to one moment of achievement. When you let go of rigid expectations—of where you should be or what you should have accomplished—you create space for unimagined possibilities.

9.2 THE WAYFINDER'S COMPASS

Change is inevitable. Change is also *not* the enemy of progress. It is the compass pointing toward uncharted opportunities. I have learned a valuable lesson throughout my career, though unfortunately it took me a long time to really absorb it: the nature of change does not define the outcome. It is how you choose to meet it. Take time to really process that thought.

Change flows through every moment, shaping our personal and professional lives. Whether we like it or not, change will happen—sometimes as a force we set in motion, sometimes as an unforeseen shift that disrupts our plans. Whether you see change as an unwelcome storm or pick up the compass it offers and let it guide you to new opportunities, the choice is yours.

Some changes are within your control: a menu update, a seasonal initiative, or a strategic shift gives you a chance to steer the narrative, to channel your vision into progress. These moments, though challenging, are yours to shape. But what about the changes you can't control? A sudden management company shake-up, a leadership team with a new direction, a trusted team member quitting without notice—all of these can feel like a tidal wave crashing against our carefully built stability. At first, these moments can feel overwhelming, even threatening. But resisting them only ties you to the past, anchoring you to what was while the tide of change pulls you further from where you need to be.

The reality is that true progress requires movement, and

movement is impossible without change. **But don't confuse movement alone with progress—it must be paired with intention.**

There is undeniable power in choosing change. Taking control of what you can doesn't just ease the grip of future uncertainty, it transforms it into momentum. During my time at L'Auberge de Sedona, this became my mantra. Introducing and collaborating on a new menu was a testament of growth and ambition, a chance to challenge the team and push ourselves to elevate our craft—a far greater aim than simply refreshing the offerings. Each seasonal menu brought with it the thrill of pairing our creative energy with precise attention to detail. The menu was not just food; it was storytelling. It entailed collaborating with my most trusted chefs to embody Sedona's beauty and the northern Arizona landscape on a plate.

I was also known for pushing tight timelines and driving the agenda for change. I have a never-ending impulse to rework menus almost as soon as they are finalized, as if I am bored of it on day one. It is not my best leadership quality—unless there is a prize for restlessness, in which case I would win, hands down. Whether it was a new holiday menu months in advance, rethinking a summer culinary experience, or weaving local flavors into our famous Sunday brunch, I constantly sought to raise the bar. Neek, my *chef de cuisine* at the time, was always the first to jump on board with me. No matter how ambitious the timeline or how last-minute the change, he was there, eyes forward, hands ready. He never resisted. At least, not out loud.

Years later, after we had both moved on and during one of our catch-up calls, we found ourselves reminiscing about old times. "Chef," he said, "you know I was always on board. I believed in the vision. But man...you were hard to keep up with. You were on another level."

His comment stuck with me. He didn't say it with resentment. I believe it was admiration, laced with a truth I had been blind to at the time. As I reflected on his words, I realized I had built momentum so strong that even my most loyal chefs had to sprint just to stay in step. And no one told me. They were too busy trying to meet the standard, trying not to let me, or themselves, down. That moment taught me something I had not learned in the kitchen: change can be a powerful compass, but only if you take the time to look around and make sure no one is getting lost in the process.

For much of my career, I was cursed, it seemed, with a near-constant question on my mind: *What's next?* I was not content with staying the same. I needed to set a new vision, to embrace the next challenge, to constantly recreate with a relentless commitment to excel and perform. By choosing change, I created direction, setting the stage for evolution rather than waiting for stagnation to creep in. There was a lesson there: when I leaned into change, I got to set the course. I gained clarity on the next step rather than waiting for circumstances to dictate my path, my story. Change became my compass, and I became the wayfinder.

But not all change can be planned or controlled. At L'Auberge de Sedona, change was not an occasional disruption—it was a constant. The executive team was in perpetual motion, with new Directors of Sales and Marketing, General Managers, Directors of Finance, and Directors of Human Resources cycling in and out at such a ludicrous pace that it felt impossible to build a steady rhythm. Each new general manager had their own strengths, weaknesses, and "wonderful" ideas about how the resort should run. It was unsettling for us as department heads trying to adapt to their changing priorities, so you can only imagine how confusing and frustrating it must have been for the employees and the guests. Through it all, the only constants were Kristin, overseeing the rooms department, and me, managing Food & Beverage. We did our best to anchor ourselves and our teams, even as the environment around us seemed to change by the day.

Adding to the uncertainty, we knew another change in management was coming. It was a major shift on the horizon that no one could not talk about, even as it loomed over a lot of decisions. We were expected to stay focused and engaged in the present, but with so much turnover and such an unclear future, it was difficult to feel grounded. At that point, though, John—my Executive Chef—and I were almost unfazed. I remember him walking into the kitchen one morning, nodding toward the kitchen line and saying, "So, are we getting a new boss again?" with that half-smile he had when he already knew the answer. Then he tied his apron and got to work, just like he always did. We did not waste energy on what we could not control. We kept moving, kept delivering. That was the only way forward.

Change was no longer an isolated event; it was the backdrop of everything we did. At first, the constant churn of new leadership felt discouraging. Sure, some of the changes were necessary and helpful, but the ever-shifting priorities around us made it hard to focus on the work itself. It would have been easy to let frustration take over (and it did quite a few times behind closed doors) or to let the instability dictate how we showed up. But instead of resisting the changes we couldn't control, we turned inward, toward our teams, our standards, and the values that had to remain consistent no matter who was at the helm—and we did so with the undivided support of our ownership group. It was not an easy path, but it was a necessary one.

Change, especially when it is this constant, demands more than just endurance; it demands a serious dose of adaptability. Resisting it only makes it harder to navigate. Leaning into change, even when it feels inconvenient or overwhelming, is when the real growth happens.

Those years at L'Auberge de Sedona taught me how to stay steady when nothing else was. Adopting the changes taking place around us was rarely easy, but over time it became less about what we were losing and more about what I had gained in the process of navigating these changes: new perspectives, a deeper resilience, and a confidence in my ability to move forward, no matter what. I emerged from this experience with a greater sense of who I was, and, more importantly, where I was going.

The beauty of change, should we choose to embrace it, lies in its role as a compass, guiding us toward uncharted paths we might never have chosen or even imagined for ourselves before. When change arrives—whether welcomed or uninvited—it rarely feels like an opportunity at first, especially since it brings about some amount of discomfort, even pain. Yet, those moments of disruption hold the seeds of transformation within them.

This important lesson became strikingly clear to me in mid-2018, during one of the hardest changes I faced during my time in Sedona. The much-anticipated new management company, Evolution Hospitality, arrived with a massive team, not to collaborate but to take over. Their bold and unyielding approach felt judgmental and dismissive, as though our years of effort were being erased without understanding the context or the past challenges we overcame. Frustration bubbled over as they critiqued nearly everything we did without asking questions, leaving no room for conversation, only criticism. It felt less like a partnership and more like an uninvited audit. I vividly remember feeling sidelined and undervalued, a stark contrast to the collaborative environment I had tried to foster. Eventually, I could not keep my frustrations to myself. Speaking up to the new corporate team was not easy, but I felt it was necessary. To their credit, this honest confrontation seemed to shift something. Slowly, the tone began to change. Commands gave way to conversations, and what initially felt like a hostile takeover transformed into a gradual alignment of our goals.

As the dust settled, I realized we were on the same team, though it had taken time and discomfort for me to see it. Evolution Hospitality's methods, through jarring, came from a place of good intention: to push us toward something better. Their approach forced me to lean into discomposure, to advocate for my perspective, and, ultimately, to find common ground in a situation that felt anything but collaborative at first.

Through this experience, I learned once again that every pivot, every detour, and every unexpected redirection carries with it a lesson or opportunity. Change, even when it feels like a wrecking ball, remains a compass, teaching us to trust the pull, follow where it leads, and uncover hidden strengths. What may seem like a setback at first could, in fact, be a path to the next chapter of your career.

9.3 BECOMING UNFINISHED

On this journey of relentless growth, you will flip the script on the traditional idea of success by defying the finality of "perfection" as an end goal. Instead, you will be celebrating your imperfections, emphasizing the journey, breaking free from society's expectations, and learning to love the perpetual state of *becoming*.

The greatest triumph of a growth mindset is not the external accolades we receive or the milestones we pass in our careers; it's the deep, internalized understanding that we are never truly finished. That mastery is not a summit to reach but the obsessive dedication to an ongoing climb. To embrace this unfinished state is to see beauty in progress. It is to be free of others' beliefs in your abilities and what you *should* be doing. Freed from the expectation, both external and internal, to have everything figured out.

You do not need to reach perfection. What matters is that you are moving forward, little by little, one step at a time. What matters is staying open to learning. This mindset also lends perspective. When you stop viewing your professional career as a series of final destinations, you let go of the pressure to "arrive" and you start finding fulfillment in who you are becoming, not in what you achieve. And that perspective is so liberating!

To become unfinished is to embrace the paradox of growth: you are both complete in your efforts today and perpetually evolving into something greater tomorrow. This doesn't mean you are incomplete or that you're somehow flawed until you become a different version of yourself. You've entered a deliberate state of being—rooted in the recognition that growth keeps you fully engaged in the process of becoming. But this deliberate state of being requires the choice to live unfinished and shift your focus from achieving perfection to engaging with purpose. This choice frees you from the need to measure your worth against external standards and allows you to measure your growth against your own aspirations instead. You will always be pursuing a version of yourself that remains a step ahead of present-day you. That is the paradox of growth; you are both the architect and the masterpiece of your own story, always evolving yet always whole.

The early months of 2020, when the COVID-19 pandemic spread across continents, were unlike anything I or anyone else experienced before: a collision of fear, extreme doubt, responsibility, and huge uncertainty that tested every ounce of strength we had. At L'Auberge de Sedona, the impact of the global pandemic was immediate and staggering. We witnessed the world change by the day, sometimes by the hour, and it was impossible not to feel the weight of what this meant—not only for our livelihoods but for our health, our loved ones, and the very fabric of our lives. Every decision carried with it a shadow of doubt: *What if I get exposed? What if I bring this home?* These were not abstract concerns; they were real and urgent. The virus was invisible, silent, and, for too many, merciless. With no vaccine available yet, protocols were stringent for those who chose to adhere to them, while other, more stubborn individuals dismissed them entirely, showing a lack of regard for the potential impact of their choices on others' health. Quarantine became a part of our life—mandatory, isolating, and necessary. If someone showed symptoms, or if they were simply exposed to someone with the virus, they had to isolate themselves immediately. Sometimes that meant weeks alone in a hotel room, waiting for test results that could take up to fourteen days to arrive. The uncertainty during those days was maddening. I was not just quarantining; I was holding my breath, hoping I had not inadvertently carried the virus to someone I cared about, especially to my wife, whom we had just found out was pregnant with our first child.

The weight of responsibility was enormous. As the number of cases grew, we began to scale back operations. Week by week, we reduced staff until we went from a bustling team of 240 to just a dozen of us keeping the lights on. I was tasked with deciding who to keep in Food & Beverage—decisions I agonized over as the team became smaller and smaller. I knew that every person I sent home would face weeks, maybe months, of doubt and uncertainty with no guarantee of a return. These people were not just colleagues at this point—they were my team, they were people I had worked alongside, laughed with, and built incredible memories with.

The resort itself became eerily quiet. Some days, we had just one room occupied. It felt almost post-apocalyptic. But I had to press on, balancing minimal operations with the constant anxiety of exposure. Every interaction carried a risk since we knew so little about the virus. There was no escape from it. Every cough, every headache made us pause and wonder.

In the thick of this, I depended heavily on my growth mindset. It was not about staying optimistic—there was no room for blind hope. I felt a responsibility to be resilient and continue forward, even when the way forward felt impossible. I leaned on the belief that we could adapt, even when the conditions felt unbearable.

As we slowly began to reopen, the challenges shifted but never disappeared. Occupancy would rise but staffing lagged. We were always behind, asked by management to prove that we were overwhelmed and completely swamped before we could justify bringing back more staff. It was frustrating, nonsensical, and unsettling. On top of that, the pace was crazy, with sixteen-plus-hour days, many of them on our own. Every day required such a delicate balance between caution and action, between taking care of immediate needs, thinking long-term, and *being your own solution*.

Looking back, I see those months as some of the most challenging of my career. The global pandemic exposed how unfinished we all are—how much we need to rely on each other and how vital it is to embrace the unknown as a constant state, not an exception. It was, for many, a time of loss, learning, and reflection. And I hope it is an experience no one has to relive in their lifetime. Still, I am grateful for the lessons it taught me about the need to persevere and the acceptance required to continue growing through the darkest of times.

CHAPTER 10

EMBRACING LIFELONG GROWTH

This is it—the last chapter. If you've made it to this point, you already understand that growth—true *relentless* growth—never really ends. But before you close this book for good, I want to cover a few more things, ideas that are integral to carrying this mindset forward. Think of this as your final preparation before taking off on your own, with your newfound knowledge, tools, and principles to guide you. The door to possibility is open, and I want you to remember: this is your story, your growth. You now have the ability to create and pursue your own path, and I hope these final pages leave you inspired, grounded, and ready to take on whatever comes next.

10.1 JUST LIKE AN ORIGINAL SOUNDTRACK

From as far back as I can remember, movies were more than entertainment to me—they were magic. As a child, I was captivated by the stories unfolding before me on the big screen. But what truly elevated those stories—what made my heart race and my eyes widen, what made me sit on the very edge of my seat—was the music. And no composer stirred my emotions quite like Hans Zimmer.

I can still picture the first time his music truly hit me. It was not just a background score; it was a character all on its own. Whether it was the thunderous battle cries of *Gladiator*, the temporal mastery of *Interstellar*, or the magnificence of *The Lion King*, I loved it. Mufasa's scene? Nine-year-old me in 1994 went through all the stages of grief...twice. These compositions did not just accompany the scenes—they defined them. As I grew, my love for movies only deepened. Cinema became my sanctuary, a place where I could lose myself and find myself all at once.

I still have such admiration for Hans Zimmer. His masterpieces rarely rely on sudden bursts or dramatic flourishes to command attention. Instead, his scores unfold gradually, layer by layer, building tension and emotion in ways that feel both inevitable and surprising. His compositions invite you in; they do not demand your focus.

Similar to Zimmer's compositions, growth takes shape in the small, deliberate choices we make each day. It emerges as a quiet, persistent invitation to approach our work with attention, to nurture our relationships with intention, and to respond to setbacks with grace and persistence. Over time, this rhythm of effort and intention builds—just like an original soundtrack—until we find ourselves transformed, at the height of progress. Then, once again, our relentless growth fades into the background.

Sometimes growth is a crescendo, but it's always the steady beat beneath everything, quietly driving our actions with subtle consistency. Other times, its pace quickens, demanding attention and effort, pushing us to rise to challenges we didn't anticipate. Yet, no matter the tempo, growth is always there, ever in the background, reminding us that every moment holds the potential for transformation.

Growth is such a deeply personal journey. It is not something that can be handed to you or imposed by others. It is something you actively shape, because it's uniquely yours to define and nurture. It can be a lonely journey because no two paths are the same, but this very individuality is what makes progress so meaningful. You and you alone know exactly where you've been and where you want to go. But at times, your progress can feel invisible. You will wonder if the small steps you're taking are leading anywhere or if the challenges you've faced have set you too far back. When you find yourself pondering this, ask yourself: Are the actions I'm taking today moving me closer to the person I want to become? You might not get an immediate answer, but introspection at least creates the space to connect with your progress in a way that feels both personal and intentional.

And intention is what growth thrives on. Without it, the journey becomes aimless—you're moving forward but without understanding why. With it, you bring energy to your growth, and that energy determines how far you will go. Show up to your life and your work with purpose, knowing that even the smallest actions shape the bigger picture of your progress. This intentionality ensures that your progress aligns with your forward focus and isn't simply random movement in any direction. Instead, each step you take will reflect who you are and what you value.

In many ways, this process of relentless growth mirrors the essence of hospitality. The guest rarely notices the preparation behind a seamless experience—the small, deliberate actions that elevate service into something unforgettable. The same is true for growth. The effort might not always be visible, even to yourself, but it is there, building momentum in the background. Just like a thoughtful touch in hospitality leaves a lasting impression, the intention you bring to your growth journey ensures that it becomes something sustainable and natural—an undeniable part of your life and career.

Consistent growth also thrives on reflection. When you take the time to pause and consider how far you've come, what's working and what's not, you create the clarity needed to move forward with confidence. Remember, there is purpose in the pause—not just after a setback or when redefining a "failure," but at any point when you find yourself questioning your progress. These moments of self-reflection are never wasted; they are where growth takes root. We need to pause, especially in a rushing world full of impatience, pressuring us toward external metrics of success. So please, take the time to pause, think, and reflect on your journey. You may realize you've come much further than you thought.

Self-reflection often begins with the quiet acknowledgement that where we are today is not where we will be tomorrow. During the COVID-19 pandemic—a time when the world itself seemed to pause—we were each given a rare chance to reassess our priorities. I found myself unable, as usual, to simply stand still during that time. While everything around me was put on hold, I was still committed to the craft and working in the industry that shaped me. I could not resist seeing this period as an unusual opening to envision a future version of myself, one slightly different from who I was at that moment. This realization did not come lightly. It required confronting some rather uncomfortable questions: *What impact do I want to create in the lives of others beyond my current role? How can I challenge myself to grow while staying aligned with what truly fulfills me?* I wanted to find a way to add new dimensions to who I was and what I had to offer— both in hospitality and beyond. But I knew that if I waited for the "right time" to pursue the impact I wanted to have, that "right time" might never come.

So, I chose to use what little spare time I had during 2019 to study and develop skills to become a certified coach, speaker, and trainer. Initially, this endeavor felt a bit daunting, but being able to learn and study at my own pace made it manageable, especially because I was still working full time during the pandemic. The value of investing in my future self kept me grounded, and as I began the certification program, my purpose became even clearer. I felt a deep pull to lay the groundwork for my future as though the timing *was* right, even if the full plan hadn't yet taken shape. I made a quiet commitment to myself to be prepared, making sure that when the next chapter arrived I would be able to meet whatever opportunity came calling. As I approached the final six months before my certification, I took an even bolder step: I began building my own company from the ground up.

Entrepreneurship opened up an entirely new world—one I felt I had no business being in. It was complicated and confusing, demanding creativity, resilience, and a strong willingness to learn as I went. From writing my business plan to building a brand, every detail required attention: setting up the website, defining my core values, writing the mission statement, and so much more. My schedule grew tighter than ever. And whose fault was it? Yet again, I had chosen to answer the constant "What's next?" playing out in my mind, and I was feeling the growing pains. There were moments when it felt like too much—juggling my work in hospitality in the middle of a pandemic, hours of study, and the demands of launching a business. But I kept showing up, driven by the vision of what this growth could mean for my future.

Through the process of building my company I learned

something fundamental: embracing lifelong growth often requires pursuing what feels right, even if the steps are not fully defined. I had to see the potential for growth and change as an invitation to start now. And that decision was transformative, not because it changed what I did, but because it reshaped who I saw in myself; I am always evolving, always learning, and always ready to adapt. That is how I came to see myself, and with the creation of Incrementum, my company, my story of growth took a huge step forward. Incrementum means growth, and everything about my entrepreneurial journey has felt right, as if the path has been there for me all along.

Like an original Hans Zimmer soundtrack, it started with a single note, quiet yet full of intention, building layer by layer into something greater—possibly becoming a masterpiece, who knows? This progress has its own steady rhythm, ever in the background, always pulling me forward.

10.2 THE PATH IS YOURS

At this point, you know what relentless growth demands: vision, resilience, adaptability, and the patience to endure. Now the path shifts. What comes next is uncharted, yours to define, navigate, and shape. There is no map and no safety net; there are no guarantees. That is the beauty of it. The question at the core of a growth mindset is not "What will you achieve?" but "Who will you become?" Your journey is no longer about checking off milestones. It's about how you show up each day—seeking meaning, staying curious, and refusing to settle for mediocrity. Growth is no longer something you pursue but something you embody, never-ending and ever-present, something you live out through the course of your professional journey.

When I arrived at the Mayflower Inn & Spa in Washington, Connecticut, in 2021, I walked into an environment where the bar of excellence was practically out of reach, by design. The town of Washington itself felt almost untouched by time: quaint, pristine, and remote. No-cell-phone-tower remote. Nestled in Litchfield County, it's a quiet escape for those seeking beauty and serenity. Rolling hills, lush greenery, and a sense of exclusivity define the area. For those unfamiliar with its charm, Washington, CT, is where people go to disappear from the noise of the world, to retreat into understated luxury.

At the center of this idyllic landscape stands the Mayflower Inn & Spa, a cornerstone of refined hospitality. With its timeless New England architecture and gardens that look like something out of a painting, the property evokes a feeling of stepping into another era, where everything is deliberate, every detail flawless. This was not just any resort; it was a part of Auberge Resorts Collection, one of the top hospitality brands in the world. Auberge is synonymous with excellence, and the Mayflower did not disappoint. It was clearly not competing with other luxury resorts; it was setting the bar.

Mayflower Inn & Spa had just undergone a major renovation

when I arrived. Everything was fresh, elegant, and ready to be shown off, but with that came immense pressure. Every corner of the property—from the tranquil spa, "The Well," to the meticulously designed rooms—had been curated to offer guests a world-class experience. And I was responsible for making sure that experience extended to every plate, every service, every event, and every moment guests spent with us.

Guests were paying upwards of $2,000 a night for the privilege of staying there. Expectations were not just high, they were stratospheric. The Food & Beverage program had been reimagined to deliver a robust and immersive culinary experience. The bar had been set aggressively high, with ambitious programming and an equally aggressive budget to match. But the reality behind the scenes told a different story. There was an unhealthy culture in Food & Beverage; toxic leadership had eroded trust and a nearly nonexistent staff was exhausted whenever they were there. The banquet and catering operation was about to tackle a level of business they had never seen before, with big events on the books but no processes, systems, or procedures in place to properly execute them.

I remember one moment in particular; it happened on a Saturday during peak season. We had a wedding event that included a ceremony on the lawn, cocktail hour in the Shakespeare Garden, and dinner under a custom tent on the far end of the twenty-three-acre property. It sounds beautiful, and it was; but operationally it was pure madness. The main kitchen was in the historic Mayflower Cottage, nowhere near where we needed to serve over one hundred plated dinners on time, at the right temperature, with the level of finesse that Auberge Resort Collection demands. We had to move everything—hot boxes, speed racks, all the mise en place—across uneven paths with stairs and manicured lawns, loading equipment, prep, and production into the trunks of our cars. There was no banquet kitchen on that side of the property. Just us, trying to build a pop-up restaurant in what felt like the middle of nowhere.

At one point, I found myself running back and forth on a golf cart to the main inn, sweating through my uniform, dodging another golf cart carrying the bride's grandmother, and hearing from my banquet captain that the plated course needed to be pushed because the reception was running long. The food was ready. The timing was not. And there we were, standing under our "kitchen" tent, lined up like we were about to go on stage, praying it all held together.

Not a single guest knew the pressure we were under or the finesse it took to pull off that night successfully. They just raved about the food, the flow, the elegance. But for us? We had teetered on the edge of chaos and executed with precision. That is what it took to operate at that level. That was our Mayflower standard.

Being there felt like getting the keys to a luxury race car without an engine and being told, or should I say expected, to win the race. The challenge was unlike anything I had faced before.

I found myself wondering if the team even believed success was possible at that property. There was no room for mediocrity, no space for excuses. Each day, each meal period, each experience carried the weight of expectation—a promise of excellence that we could not afford to break. Food & Beverage was the heartbeat of it all, yet most days it felt like we were running on fumes.

I needed to define what my path would be on this remote and difficult to staff property. I had faced pressure in my career before, but this was different. I had no map, no safety net, and no guarantee of success. Every day brought new challenges, and with so much at stake, staying on track felt nearly impossible. There were so many moments where chaos seemed to be winning— staffing shortages, impossible demands, expectations that doubled every time I turned around. Finding talent was a constant battle. I had to rely on my relationships, network, and kindness toward the existing staff to spread the word and bring people in through referrals. We were not in a bustling city where professionals were plentiful; we were tucked away in a small town where people valued quiet and simplicity, and some staff members had to drive up to forty-five minutes to come to work. It was hard, at first, to convince anyone to sign up for the intensity that lay ahead. But one thing was certain: I could not face this challenge alone—no one could.

So, I made a few calls, and soon John, Neek, and Miranda joined me. When I think of what it means to have a real team— one that doesn't flinch under pressure, doesn't get distracted by noise, doesn't fold when the weight gets too heavy—I immediately think of them. They are reliable and battle-tested. The kind of people who show up, not for the spotlight but for the standard. And show up they did.

John was my right arm. We had a rhythm, one built on mutual trust, earned over years of hard service. He was an exceptional culinarian, sharp on execution, and one of the hardest workers I've ever known. Always tired, and not shy about saying it, but he never stopped. You could see it on his face; exhaustion lived in his eyes, but when the service turned into a blood bath, John would still be standing next to the team, wiping down the pass, ready to go again. He never let me down. Not once. He anchored the kitchen, and more often than not, he anchored me too.

Neek was a natural force; the one who would run into the fire first, not because he had to but because he knew it had to be done. He pushed the team forward even when we had nothing left to give, and somehow still managed to bring everyone with him. He had this drive that was both grounding and contagious. You could see it in the way he spoke to the line: direct, fast, but never flustered. He kept standards high without raising his voice, and the cooks respected him because they knew he was right there with them. He made people believe it could be done, even when logic said otherwise. And more often than not, it got done because of him.

And Miranda, she was the quiet force. The calm within the storm. Her precision, her sense of pride, and her refusal to compromise made the pastry program feel like it belonged in its own league. She was focused under pressure, every single day. There was a steadiness to her that never wavered, no matter what the day threw at us. I could walk into her kitchen mid-crisis— staff call outs, busy day all around, timing tight—and she would be there, cool as ever, finishing her preparation work with the same focus, as if we had all the time in the world. Without saying much, she would always hand me something sweet to taste; just enough to keep me going. It was her quiet way of looking out for me. She did not need the spotlight to lead; she led by the way she showed up. Her work was detailed, beautiful, thoughtful. But more than that, it was consistent. In an environment where pressure could swallow people whole, Miranda was a reminder that excellence could be quiet. She did not just carry the pastry program, she elevated it.

We were understaffed, overcommitted, and expected to produce a level of luxury that did not allow for excuses. And somehow, with them by my side, we delivered. They allowed me to lead boldly. To push harder. To expect more. Because I knew they had my back—not with words but with action. And that is what made them the best. Not talent alone, not titles, but their heart, their grit, their refusal to settle, and their commitment to relentless growth.

Looking back, I have worked with a lot of teams. Good ones. Strong ones. But this crew? They were different. They were the real ones. The people I trusted implicitly. They had been in the trenches with me before, and they knew what it took to succeed under fire. There was no doubt in my mind that with them by my side I could go to war. We built systems where barely any existed; we found and trained one of the best teams in business, in the restaurant, and in the kitchen; and we created something that lived up to the Mayflower's name.

It was far from easy. Every day tested our limits, and we fought hard for every win. What I learned in those beginning months at the Mayflower Inn & Spa was this: at times, you are on your own—no instructions, no blueprint, and no safety net to rely on. But with the right people, an obsessive commitment, and a refusal to settle for anything less than extraordinary, even the impossible starts to feel achievable. And for a place like the Mayflower Inn & Spa—where luxury is the standard—nothing less would do.

Here is something worth remembering: leadership has nothing to do with title. It is not reserved for executives, managers, or those with authority over others. Leadership is not a proclamation, it's a way of acting and serving that begins with serving yourself. Not selfishly, but intentionally. By first holding yourself accountable, showing up with integrity, and staying committed to growth, you set the tone for everything you do and for everyone on your team. Leading your own life and career is the ultimate form of self-respect. It entails making choices based on what matters most, not on what is easiest. It is serving your purpose, pushing yourself when you would rather stay comfortable, and staying disciplined when no one is watching.

This is servant leadership in its rawest form: being someone who leads by example, holds themselves to a high standard, and earns trust—beginning with their own. Whether you're leading a team or simply interacting with guests, true leadership is about service. You must lift up those around you by showing up fully yourself, listening actively, and creating space for growth, both for yourself and others. A servant leader does not climb over people to get ahead. They bring others along for the climb, embodying the belief that growth does not have to be a solo act.

No one else will walk your path for you. You must decide for yourself what direction you will go, what values matter most, where to focus your energy, and how you want to balance ambition with professional fulfillment. And you absolutely must understand *why* you are doing it all. You have learned the tools, the processes, and the mindset required for the path ahead, but the next steps you take are *entirely yours*. Growth will not force itself upon you. No one will push you to lead *your* journey. You must choose to take the lead. Act like a leader, whether or not anyone calls you one. Lead yourself with humility, serve others with empathy, and carry your mindset of relentless growth forward. Take ownership of the struggles, the choices, and the victories that await. The path may be uncertain, but your purpose is not. You do not need a title to lead—you just need the courage to act. This journey has always been yours.

So, who will you become?

10.3 BEYOND THE FINAL PAGE

I want you to pause with me for a moment and imagine we are sitting together, sharing a conversation like old friends. The noise of the world fades away and it's just us in this stillness.

I see how far you have come. I can see it in the way you carry yourself, in the strength behind your questions, the intention behind your word choices and actions. Maybe you feel it too, that quiet sense of accomplishment, like a seed finally taking root. Or maybe it is still settling in, elusive and hard to grasp, and that is okay too.

I want you to know something: what you have built within yourself—the resilience, the grit, the clarity—it is real. It is not fleeting, not something that can be undone by a bad day, a mistake, or a moment of self-doubt. This foundation is yours. It is yours because you earned it, and because you are still earning it, brick by brick.

This chapter may be ending, but your story is not. *Relentless growth* has no final act; it is a continuum. The mindset you have cultivated is a compass for the road ahead. Where it takes you is entirely up to you.

For the seasoned leader who came here looking to reignite your passion, perhaps you have rediscovered that spark. Maybe you have a deeper understanding of why you started this journey in the first place. Remember, you can choose to be the guide, the anchor, and the inspiration for those around you. The growth mindset you have embraced is not just for you; it is a gift to be shared with your team, your peers, and those who look to you for guidance. As you consider what's next, ask yourself: *What can you give? How can you lead with renewed purpose?* Your impact will ripple far beyond anything you can see today. Believe me, I have seen it and I have lived it.

For the emerging leader, this is your time to rise. You may still be figuring out your place in the professional world, testing your abilities, and learning where you want to go. That is completely okay. With every step forward, you're building a stronger foundation. Take what you have learned here and let it guide you as you carve your own path. Growth will challenge you, but it will also reward you with opportunities to become the kind of leader you have always admired—one who leads with vision, integrity, and obsessive determination. So, let me ask you: *What will you create with this mindset? What kind of future will you build?*

And last but not least, to the hospitality student or newcomer to this field: Welcome! Know that your journey is just beginning. The principles of growth, resilience, and adaptability that you're learning are as crucial in the kitchen, on the floor, and behind the scenes as they are in your everyday life. This industry will test you in ways you can't yet imagine. But it will also shape you, push you, and reward you in ways that are profoundly fulfilling. Let your curiosity guide you, and never stop asking how you can grow—not just for the guest experience or the team but for yourself. I'll leave you with these questions: *What is next for you? Where will this mindset take you as you navigate the highs and lows of this incredible industry?*

There is always time for one last story, so I'll share it now. On January 6, 2023, I received a message from my general manager asking me to meet him in his office. I knew the tone; it was formal, not his usual style. Still, I was not totally prepared for what came next. My position at the Mayflower Inn & Spa was being eliminated. Just like that.

For a moment, I could not speak. The words hit like a blunt object. I sat across from him in silence, trying to process. For two years, we had built something truly remarkable—something rare. I had created a team I trusted implicitly and an operation that was both successful and sustainable. We had rebuilt the resort's food and beverage culture from the inside out. Turnover was minimal, morale was high, and the kitchen had rhythm even on our toughest days. There was no screaming, no ego battles, no revolving door of employees. Just work, pride, and consistency. It wasn't perfect, nothing ever is in hospitality, but it was thriving. And I was proud of that. So when the words came—"position eliminated"—something in me severed.

I walked out of that office with a tightness in my chest.

Everything looked the same—the hallway, the candles in the lounge, the scent of warm apple cider from the tap room drifting through the air—but everything felt different. My first thought was about the team. *How would they take it? How would I stand in front of people who had given me their trust, their time, their belief, and tell them I couldn't stay, all because a decision was made without me?* Gathering them in the garden room, looking them in the eye, telling them what happened without letting the emotion crack my voice was one of the hardest meetings of my career.

And then there was Kristin. The car ride home that day felt like the longest drive of my life. With my hands on the wheel, I rehearsed what I would say, how I would say it. Not because I didn't think she would understand but because I was still trying to understand it myself. *How do you explain losing something that looked, felt, and functioned like success?*

We had bought a house just over a year prior, and I did not want this to rip through the life we were building. But Kristin—my rock—stepped in with strength and unhesitating support. She held us together while I wrestled with the uncertainty ahead. She sent me job applications to look at, encouraged me to stay focused, and reminded me that we would figure it out...together. What began as the biggest professional setback of my life became my greatest blessing. Faced with no fallback, I dusted off Incrementum, my consulting company that had been sitting quietly on the sidelines since our move to Connecticut. I expanded its scope to include Food & Beverage and culinary consulting and fully committed to entrepreneurship, a path I did not feel ready for but one that life had clearly chosen for me, and one that I knew my growth mindset would help me travel down, learning as I went.

I reached out to my network, sending exactly fifty-three emails. Sixteen responses came back—positive and encouraging—but the truth was that I needed more than encouragement; I needed a job. Finally, a single opportunity came through, and I seized it like my life depended on it. That moment, though humbling, was the launchpad for everything that followed.

This chapter of my life taught me that sometimes the biggest changes come just when you think you're done writing your story, and you may be forced to rewrite the script entirely.

I never expected to embrace entrepreneurship as quickly as I did, and yet, here I am—grateful beyond words for that job elimination. Without it, I would not have had the chance to spend these precious, transformative years raising my two daughters, Lorena and Camila. I would not be here for their milestones, their laughter, or those irreplaceable moments of togetherness.

Sometimes life doesn't ask you if you are ready, it just assumes you are and it shows you where you're supposed to go next.

As we end our time together, I'll leave you with this: look at each new beginning as a chance to test the depth of your character. Lean into the unknown with curiosity, knowing that the answers often reveal themselves through the journey, not before it begins. You have cultivated a mindset that thrives on progress and the willingness to learn, unlearn, and relearn as the circumstances demand.

Maybe our paths will cross again. Maybe there is more to explore together. But for now, it's time for you to step forward knowing you're equipped to write your own next chapter. You are not alone on this journey; the principles shared here connect you to countless others who are also navigating their paths with intention, determination, and the relentless thirst to grow.

So go forward with confidence. Trust the process when uncertainty arises, and embrace it as an invitation to grow further. Celebrate not just the peaks but also those moments of unseen effort, for they are what define true progress. And most importantly, never stop growing. Because your story is far from over.

See you at work...

ACKNOWLEDGMENTS

To my rock, my wife Kristin. Your love and commitment to our family ground me every day. You have been by my side through it all, you love me in spite of myself, and I would not be here without you. To my daughters, Lorena and Camila, you are a toddler and an infant as I am writing this book; accept it as a piece of me that I hope you will cherish forever. It is a glimpse into my journey, written with you both in my heart while watching you both grow up to be my greatest gifts in life.

A mes parents, Maman et Papa, merci de m'avoir soutenu tout au long de ma carrière professionnelle et, plus important encore, de m'avoir permis de suivre ma passion dès l'âge de 14 ans. Votre confiance en moi m'a donné le courage de poursuivre cette voie et a mis en place les bases de la vie que j'ai construite.

Throughout this process, I have been fortunate to have incredible support. Yannick Law, Mark Jones, and Ryan Swanson, your feedback, encouragement, and belief in me have been invaluable. Suzie Yang, your wisdom and kindness have always been a guiding force, and Brad Harvey, your support has been a cornerstone of my book-writing journey. Chad Pacheco, I will never forget how you helped me see clearly when I was completely stuck in Chapter 6; with one conversation you cleared away a month of roadblocks. Mahalo. And Antwon Brinson, witnessing your growth and entrepreneurial journey has been a truly inspiring reminder of what is possible.

I also owe thanks to those who did not believe in me, the naysayers who pushed me to see another path forward. To the so-called "leaders" who became obstacles to my growth, you taught me something invaluable: I could outwork you, outgrow you, and continue my journey on my terms.

And finally, to my book coach, Sabrina Butler. This book would not exist without your guidance. What could have taken a decade (or never seen the light of day) became a reality because of your insight and encouragement.

To each of you, and to everyone who has been a part of this journey, thank you. Your impact is felt on every page of this book. Thank you. Mahalo. Merci.

ABOUT THE AUTHOR

Franck Desplechin has been a distinguished figure in the world of Culinary and Food & Beverage operations for over 25 years. His exceptional leadership acumen and expertise stem from his unstoppable commitment to personal and professional growth. Throughout his illustrious career in the kitchens of several Michelin-star-rated restaurants in France and some of the most luxurious brands around the world, such as St. Regis Hotels & Resorts and Auberge Resort Collection, Franck has exemplified flexibility and adaptability, seamlessly aligning with organizational needs while spearheading teams to unprecedented success. His tenure is marked by a striking track record of coaching, delivering, and implementing development-focused leadership while flawlessly integrating into the existing workplace culture.

Franck's unique journey started at the school of hard knocks when he decided to work in kitchens at 14 years old instead of going to high school. His "neurotic" obsession to keep moving forward against all odds and adversities has earned him recognition as a true mastermind in his field. He is a firm believer that adopting a professional growth mindset will transform an individual to reach career fulfillment.

Affable yet commanding, Franck embodies the essence of an accomplished mentor, motivational teacher, and servant-leader. His charismatic and confident demeanor has left an indelible mark on those fortunate enough to work alongside him. Franck's leadership philosophy is transparent and direct, fostering trust and empowerment within his teams. His collaborative approach inspires and propels individuals to exceed their own expectations, elevating both performance and morale to new ground. Countless individuals have benefitted from his guidance, finding professional growth and ultimately reaching the pinnacle of their careers by becoming Executive Chefs, Directors of Food & Beverage, or venturing into restaurant ownership.

Franck Desplechin is not just a leader; he is a mentor, a visionary, and a transformer of culture. His diverse contributions to the landscape of hospitality are evidenced by obtaining Michelin stars in restaurants and being awarded the esteemed Forbes 5-star rating in hotels and resorts. His legacy is the lasting impact he has had on countless hospitality professionals who now find themselves in the same relentless pursuit of growth he has modeled his entire life.

Franck founded, owns, and operates a premier hospitality consultancy renowned for its unconventional business approach. When he is not traveling to assist hotels and resorts around the country, he enjoys hiking the trails of Connecticut with his wife Kristin and his two daughters, Lorena and Camila.

Thank You.

If you made it here, it means you care about your own growth, and that truly matters.

Keep questioning. Keep building. Keep showing up, especially when it is hard. This path is not always clear, but it is only yours to shape.

If any part of this book sparked something in you, let's stay connected. You can find me at cheffranck.com or on Instagram and LinkedIn.

Stay relentless. See you at work...

Scan the QR code to visit cheffranck.com